DATE DUE

CRIMINAL JUSTICE

Crime Fighting and Crime Prevention

CRIMINAL JUSTICE

CRIMINAL JUSTICE

Crime Fighting and Crime Prevention

Michael Newton

CHELSEA HOUSE
PUBLISHERS
An imprint of Infobase Publishing

CRIMINAL JUSTICE: Crime Fighting and Crime Prevention

Chelsea House
An imprint of Infobase Publishing
132 West 31st Street
New York NY 10001

Library of Congress Cataloging-in-Publication Data
Newton, Michael, 1951-
Crime fighting and crime prevention / Michael Newton.
    p. cm. — (Criminal justice)
Includes bibliographical references and index.
ISBN-13: 978-1-60413-629-6 (hardcover : alk. paper)
ISBN-10: 1-60413-629-4 (hardcover : alk. paper) 1. Law enforcement.
2. Crime prevention. 3. Criminal justice, Administration of. 4. Law enforcement-
United States. 5. Crime prevention—United States. 6. Criminal justice, Administration
of—United States. I. Title.
HV7921.N49 2010
363.2'30973—dc22
2009044988

Text design by Erika K. Arroyo
Cover design by Keith Trego
Composition by EJB Publishing Services
Cover printed by Bang Printing, Brainerd, MN
Book printed and bound by Bang Printing, Brainerd, MN
Date printed: April 2010

Printed in the United States of America

10 9 8 7 6 5 4 3 2 1

This book is printed on acid-free paper.

Contents

Introduction

Americans enjoy a love-hate relationship with crime. They fear personal injury and loss but treat some of their worst outlaws as folk heroes, from the bank-robbing Jesse James and Dalton brothers to murderous gangsters Al Capone and John Gotti. Even serial killers get the celebrity treatment, from Texarkana's unknown "Moonlight Murderer" of 1946 (subject of a popular film, *The Town That Dreaded Sundown,* in 1976) to Jeffrey Dahmer in the 1990s. Man-eating psychiatrist Hannibal Lecter and homicidal criminologist Dexter Morgan rank among the most popular fictional characters of modern times.

Crime and its suppression have concerned public figures throughout history. Four centuries before the Roman Empire collapsed into chaos, Seneca the Elder (54 B.C.–39 A.D.) warned his fellow citizens that "He who does not prevent a crime when he can, encourages it." Roman emperor Marcus Aurelius (121–180) declared that "Poverty is the mother of crime."[1]

British historian Henry Thomas Buckle (1821–62) blamed society itself for criminal behavior, when he said, "Society prepares the crime, the criminal commits it." Justice Louis Brandeis (1856–1941), who served on the U.S. Supreme Court from 1916 until 1939, seemed to agree, saying, "Crime is contagious. If the government becomes a law breaker, it breeds contempt for the law."[2]

On April 5, 1968, one day after a sniper murdered civil rights leader Martin Luther King Jr. (1929–68), Senator Robert Kennedy (1925–68)—brother of assassinated President John F. Kennedy (1917–63)—

addressed "the mindless menace of violence in America which again stains our land and every one of our lives." He said, "It is not the concern of any one race. The victims of the violence are black and white, rich and poor, young and old, famous and unknown. They are, most important of all, human beings whom other human beings loved and needed. No one—no matter where he lives or what he does—can be certain who will suffer from some senseless act of bloodshed. And yet it goes on and on and on in this country of ours."[3]

One month later, in Los Angeles, an assassin's bullets claimed Kennedy's life.

The plague of crime—not only "mindless violence," but every kind of criminal behavior—threatens civilized society from its small-town roots to the pinnacle of international relations. Local crimes harm individuals and families, bankrupt small businesses, and raise the taxes paid for law enforcement. Crime syndicates and corrupt corporations bribe government officials, loot banks and public treasuries, while poisoning the environment. In extreme cases, such as Yugoslavia in the 1990s or Russia and Somalia today, crime paralyzes the ability of governments to keep their people safe, while thieves and outlaw warlords rule the roost.

Crime has preoccupied Americans from Plymouth Rock to 9/11 and beyond. The problem will not go away, but new means of investigating and restricting crime are constantly pursued in every state and nation of the world. The measures taken to combat crime may define particular societies, their hopes and goals, and the relationship between their governments and citizens.

Chapter 1, "The Crime War," reveals the impact of crime on modern America and looks at the broad range of organizations created to suppress it.

Chapter 2, "The History of Crime," traces the history of crime-control efforts from ancient times to the 21st century, including evolution of criminal laws and police agencies.

Chapter 3, "Local Police," examines the history, jurisdiction, and crime-fighting role of law enforcement agencies at the municipal and county levels.

Chapter 4, "State Police," charts the development of American state police, reviews their jurisdiction, and investigates their tactics.

As Attorney General, Robert F. Kennedy dedicated his life to fighting crime. *AP Photo*

Chapter 5, "The Feds," presents the history and operations of federal law enforcement agencies from George Washington's appointment of the first U.S. Marshals through changes spawned by modern terrorist attacks.

Chapter 6, "Crime Beyond Borders," provides an overview of international law and the agencies that enforce it against criminals worldwide.

Chapter 7, "Helping Ourselves," tracks the development of civilian crime-prevention programs, from early frontier vigilantism to modern neighborhood crime-fighting efforts.

Chapter 8, "Crime and the Media," covers the media response to crime, ranging from glorification of selected "public enemies" to participation in their capture, including the debate over fictional violence as a cause of crime.

The Crime War

Pittsburgh, Pennsylvania

At 6:00 A.M on November 19, 2008, agents of the Federal Bureau of Investigation (FBI) raided the home of Robert Korbe, one of 35 Pittsburgh residents indicted on charges of distributing cocaine between October 2007 and September 2008. During that raid, Agent Samuel Hicks was shot and killed. Between 1991 and 2007, Robert Korbe twice pled guilty to drug and weapons charges, receiving probation each time. When the raid occurred, he was free on bond pending trial on new charges of cocaine possession, resisting arrest, and assaulting police officers. Defense attorney Sumner Parker told reporters that his clients thought the agents were a gang of criminal home invaders, but Robert Korbe went further, claiming from jail, "They shot their own guy. I didn't shoot him." Prosecutors charged Korbe's wife Christina with murdering Agent Hicks.[1]

West Paterson, New Jersey

On December 1, 2008, agents of the U.S. Drug Enforcement Administration (DEA) arrested Alberto Olguin on charges of possessing a controlled dangerous substance with intent to distribute. Specifically, the agents seized 165 pounds of crystal methamphetamine—or "ice"— valued at $11 million. Authorities identified Olguin as a member of a Mexican crime syndicate that produces high-purity "ice" in secret

Robert Korbe is led into Allegheny County Police headquarters in Pittsburgh after being apprehended in connection with the murder of FBI Special Agent Samuel Hicks. *AP Photo/Keith Srakocic*

"super labs" for sale in the United States. At the time of his arrest, Olguin was driving a refrigerated truck filled with farm produce, which concealed his illegal drug stash. DEA spokesmen boasted of "de-icing" the Mexican gang, but illicit drug shipments continue.[2]

Birmingham, Alabama

On the day of Olguin's capture in New Jersey, another arrest rocked Alabama's largest city. FBI agents jailed Mayor Larry Langford on charges of bribery, fraud, money-laundering, tax evasion, and conspiracy, claiming that he received $236,000 in cash, designer watches and expensive clothes in return for funneling lucrative government contracts to personal friends. Also accused in the 101-count indictment were Bill Blount, a banker in Montgomery, Alabama, and political lobbyist Al LaPierre. According to the charges, Langford committed his crimes while serving as president of Jefferson County's commission, before his election as mayor in 2007. In a separate but related case, filed in April 2008, the U.S. Securities and Exchange Commission (SEC) charged Langford with accepting $156,000 in cash and services from Blount to arrange county contracts. Deborah Vance-Bowie, Langford's chief of staff, described the charges as a personal vendetta. "I've never heard of a federal office treating this administration the way we've been treated," she told reporters. "If this is not personal, it certainly looks like it is."[3]

CRIME HITS HOME

While major crimes rate banner headlines, thousands more pass unnoticed outside of local communities. The media may overlook them, but the daily toll of crime hits home from coast to coast, in every state, county, and city nationwide.

According to the FBI, Americans suffered 1,382,012 violent crimes and 9,767,915 property crimes in 2008—one crime for every 27 men, women, and children in the country. Specific violent crimes included 16,272 cases of murder or nonnegligent manslaughter, 89,000 forcible rapes or rape attempts, 441,855 robberies, and 834,885 aggravated assaults causing bodily injury. No statistics were kept for negligent manslaughter cases, such as deaths caused by drunken drivers. Police solved 45.1 percent of all known violent crimes.[4]

The FBI's list of property crimes includes burglary (unlawful entry of a building for criminal purposes), larceny or theft of any object without violence, and arson (illegal burning of a building or vehicle). The FBI keeps no tally of crimes such as check fraud, forgery, embezzlement, or confidence games. During 2007 [2008], police nationwide reported 2,222,196 burglaries, 6,588,873 thefts (including 956,846 stolen motor vehicles), and 62,807 cases of arson. Only 17.4 percent of all property crimes were solved by year's end.[5]

Larry Langford is sworn in as Birmingham, Alabama's mayor. Langford was arrested in December 2008 on federal bribery and fraud charges. *AP Photo/The Birmingham News, Joe Songer, File*

A separate list tabulates American hate crimes, defined as offenses motivated by prejudice based on race, religion, sexual orientation, ethnicity, national origin, or physical disability. The federal Hate Crime Statistics Act of 1990 requires the U.S. Attorney General to collect data on bias-motivated offenses, but it does not require state or local police to report them. In 2007 the FBI received notice of 7,624 hate crimes involving 9,006 specific offenses. (Some offenders committed more than one crime against the same victims.) Of those offenses, 5,408 were crimes against persons (ranging from intimidation to aggravated assault), and 3,579 were crimes against property (rang-ing from vandalism to robbery and arson). No observers claim that the tabulation of hate crimes is complete. Indeed, 84.7 percent of all participating law enforcement agencies denied occurrence of *any* hate crimes in 2007. Two states with long histories of racial violence, Alabama and Mississippi, harbored 52 active hate groups in 2007, yet Alabama reported only six hate crimes, while Mississippi acknowl-edged none.[6]

The FBI maintains another tally for financial crimes, including various kinds of fraud committed by "white-collar" criminals. In 2007 the bureau investigated 529 complaints of corporate fraud, which cost investors more than $1 billion. Those cases produced 183 indictments and 173 convictions, while securing $12.6 billion in restitution orders and $38.6 million in fines. At the same time, agents investigated 1,217 cases of securities and commodities fraud, producing 320 indict-ments and 289 convictions, with $1.7 billion in restitution orders, $24 million in recoveries, and $202.7 million in fines. Complaints of health care fraud launched 2,493 investigations in 2007, resulting in 839 indictments and 635 convictions, plus $1.12 billion in restitu-tions, $4.4 million in recoveries, $34 million in fines, and 308 seizures valued at $61.2 million. Complaints of mortgage fraud totaled 46,717 for the year, with losses exceeding $813 million. FBI agents investi-gated 1,204 cases, securing 321 indictments and 260 convictions, plus $595.9 million in restitutions, $21.8 million in recoveries, and $1.7 in fines. Insurance fraud costs America $80 billion per year, raising insurance costs to the average household by $300. In 2007 the FBI investigated 209 cases, obtaining 39 indictments and 47 convictions, with $27.2 million in restitutions and $427,000 in fines. Finally, 127 investigations of mass marketing fraud produced 12 indictments and 11 convictions, plus $30.6 million in restitution orders; $278,500 in recoveries; and $52,500 in fines.[7]

On the federal drug front, DEA agents made 27,780 arrests in 2007, while seizing 1,375 pounds of heroin, 211,581 pounds of cocaine, 784,238 pound of marijuana, 2,389 pounds of methamphetamine, and 5,636,305 dosage units of banned hallucinogens.[8] No national tally is available for drug arrests and seizures by state or local police.

ORDER OF BATTLE

The troops in America's crime war are the men and women of law enforcement, pledged to defend society against all forms of crime, often at risk of their lives. In 2004—the last year with full statistics available— they numbered 1,183,251, of whom 1,076,897 served state and local agencies, while 106,354 were federal agents.[9]

America's law enforcement establishment is highly diverse. The federal government includes no less than 87 police agencies, ranging from such famous bodies as the FBI, DEA, and Secret Service to obscure groups such as the Library of Congress Police and Tennessee Valley Authority Police. The 50 states support 362 agencies assigned to enforce

CONSENSUAL CRIMES

Consensual (or "victimless") crimes are illegal acts committed by consenting adults, which harm no other parties. They are generally banned on grounds of "immorality" or some offense to "public order," often ill-defined. Some such laws— like Tucson, Arizona's ban on women wearing pants, and Logan County, Colorado's rule that husbands may not kiss their wives on Sunday—are never enforced.[10] Others carry stiff penalties and may be used unfairly to harass selected groups or individuals.

Other than suicide—banned by law in many jurisdictions, though successful self-murder cannot be punished—most consensual crimes fall under the broad heading of vice, activities considered "sinful" or degrading by lawmakers who ban them. Three major areas include:

Gambling. The federal government and all 50 states have various laws that restrict betting and games of chance. Nevada was the first state to permit casino gambling, in 1931, followed by New Jersey in 1976. Today, commercial gambling in various forms (including lotteries and racetrack betting) is legal in 11 states. Native American tribes, exempt from state and federal gambling bans, operate 354 casinos on reservations in 28 states. Even in states where gambling has been legalized, various state laws. Local law enforcement is divided between 2,409 agencies at the county level (called "boroughs" in Alaska and "parishes" in Louisiana) and 4,710 municipal police departments. Another 517 police departments patrol public schools, colleges, and universities. Finally, at least 201 "special" police agencies protect airports, railroads, parks, harbors, hospitals, museums, Indian reservations, military bases, and other facilities.[11]

Those statistics make it sound as if America is positively swarming with police, but in 2007 they were outnumbered 255 to 1 by private citizens—and they are frequently outgunned. By 1995, civilians owned an estimated 223 million guns nationwide. On average, 341,000 are

however, gamblers who operate without proper licensing may be punished.[12]

Sex. The U.S. Supreme Court banned prosecution of homosexual activity between consenting adults in June 2003, but the federal government and all 50 states still maintain laws restricting other forms of consensual sex between adults. Nevada permits prostitution in selected counties, while commercial sex is banned in the other 49 states. Most states also have laws banning incest and bigamy (simultaneous marriage to multiple partners). The U.S. military and several states also punish adultery—including Michigan, where the penalty may be life imprisonment, although no adulterers have been charged since 1971. Utah bans fornication (sex between unmarried adults), another statute commonly ignored.[13]

Intoxication. The federal government and all 50 states have laws banning possession, use, or sale of certain drugs, while others are restricted to use with a doctor's prescription. Since the failure of national Prohibition, alcohol is legal throughout the country, but the drinking age is fixed by state law, and various restrictions govern when and where alcohol may be sold or consumed. Seventeen states monopolize various aspects of liquor sales. Most communities have laws banning public drunkenness as a form of "disorderly conduct," and all states punish driving while intoxicated, either by drugs or liquor.[14]

stolen from law-abiding owners every year, for use in crime or sale to other criminals.[15] Sooner or later, the police confront them.

UNDER FIRE

Police work is not America's most dangerous occupation. In 2007, with 188 officers killed on duty, it ranked ninth, behind construction (1,178 deaths), transportation (836), agriculture (573), manufacturing (392), administration (386), retailing (336), leisure occupations (251), and wholesaling (197), with mining a close 10th (181).[16] Still, with the exception of soldiers in combat, no other job carries a greater risk of death by homicide.

According to records maintained at the National Law Enforcement Officers Memorial in Washington, D.C., 18,366 police officers died on duty between 1792 and September 2009. The memorial's walls have

CRIME WAVES

The term *crime wave* refers to a rash of similar crimes occurring within a specific period, often (but not always) committed by offenders of the same type, race, age, or class. Examples from 20th-century American history include the outbreak of "Black Hand" terrorism among Italian immigrants during 1900-1910, gangland murders committed by rival bootleg gangs during Prohibition, bank robberies and kidnappings staged by notorious "public enemies" during the Great Depression, and violence by gangs of "juvenile delinquents" in the 1950s.[17]

Crime waves are commonly announced by politicians or high-ranking law enforcement officers, who call on government to "do something" about supposedly unprecedented crime rates—and who often profit from the resulting public fear, either in votes or funding for their agencies. The media also benefits from crime waves, through increased TV ratings and newspaper sales. Others who profit from a heightened fear of crime include gun dealers, private security firms, and vendors of guard dogs.

space for another 29,233 names, and are expected to be filled around the year 2050. Between 1996 and 2007, another 673,798 police officers were assaulted while on duty.[18]

The Internet's Officer Down Memorial Page (http://www.odmp. org/) constantly updates statistics for police officers killed on duty throughout the United States. According to that tabulation, the most danger-prone agencies were the New York City Police Department (with 653 officers killed by 2008); the Philadelphia Police Department (245); the Detroit Police Department (223), the California Highway Patrol (216); the Los Angeles Police Department (200), the U.S. Bureau of Alcohol, Tobacco and Firearms (185); the St. Louis Police Department (165); the Kansas City, Missouri, Police Department (119); the Metropolitan Police of Washington, D.C. (119); and the New York State Police (114). The most dangerous states, overall, were Texas (1,653

Some critics claim that most crime waves are fictional, derived by manipulating statistics. It is certainly true that more gangland murders occurred during Prohibition than at any time before or since—at least 689 in Chicago alone[19]—but modern American bandits rob many more banks in a single year than "Baby Face" Nelson and other 1930s outlaws looted in a decade. During the last three months of 2007, the Federal Bureau of Investigation recorded 1,569 traditional bank holdups, with losses of $24.5 million.[20] Exaggeration of the threat from "public enemies" in the Depression built the modern-day FBI, with greatly expanded authority, funding, and new personnel.

Some politicians base their whole careers on fighting one "menace" after another. Richard Nixon won election to the House of Representatives and the Senate by falsely accusing opponents of sympathy toward communism. In 1952, his fame for hunting "Reds" won Nixon the vice presidency, despite evidence of personal corruption. In 1968 he was elected president on promises of "law and order," coupled with a "war" against organized crime (whose leaders had supported him financially since 1946). Four years later, Nixon's own crimes sparked the Watergate scandal, which drove him from office in disgrace.[21]

deaths), California (1,458), New York (1,391), Illinois (970), Ohio (764), Pennsylvania (714), Florida (700), Missouri (623), Georgia (575), and Michigan (538). Fifty-eight percent of all duty-related deaths resulted from gunshots, stabbings, or beatings, while 42 percent were accidental or caused by job-related illness.[22]

There is, of course, another side to the American crime war. Police are not only victims of violence. They are also trained and authorized to use violence—including deadly force—under guidelines established by state and federal law. How well they exercise that duty is a matter of heated debate.

Outside of fiction, most police never participate in gunfights, but exceptions exist for every rule. Legendary Texas Ranger Frank Hamer (1884–1955) reportedly fought more than 100 battles with outlaws, killing 52 men and 1 woman and suffering 17 wounds. Others were less courageous. During Prohibition (1920–33), federal agent Clarence Pickering killed 42 alleged bootleggers, most of them unarmed. In 1948 the racist Ku Klux Klan honored Atlanta patrolman "Trigger" Nash for killing 13 African Americans "in the line of duty."[23]

No comprehensive records exist for civilians killed by police in America. The Bureau of Justice Statistics logged 8,578 alleged felons "justifiably killed" by police nationwide between 1976 and 1998, for an average of 373 killings per year. Ninety-eight percent of those killed were male, and 42 percent were in their 20s. A majority of those killed each year were white, except during 1976–78, but African Americans (12 percent of the total U.S. population) still averaged 35 percent of those killed by police in any given year.[24]

Critics note that many police shootings are "justified" on the basis of investigations conducted by the shooter's fellow officers, without independent review, and that arbitrary ranking of the dead as "felons" may misrepresent the facts of their cases. The 1994 Crime Control Act requires the U.S. Attorney General to publish annual reports on police shootings, but as with hate crimes, it does not require police to submit statistics. Where figures do exist, they are sometimes alarming. Cincinnati police shot 22 persons in 1995, killing 13, while two more died after officers sprayed them with chemical irritants. All 15 of the dead were African Americans, at least three of them unarmed. Police in central

Florida shot 81 persons, killing 37, between 1998 and 2004. Thirty-three of those shot were unarmed. Reporters also found that Florida police only reported one-fourth of their fatal shootings to the federal government between 1999 and 2002. More than three-fourths of the 47 persons killed or wounded by New Jersey police in 2007 were minorities shot by white officers. By contrast, police throughout all of Great Britain killed only 48 persons between 1990 and 2008.[25]

Clearly, the crime war in America is dangerous for all concerned.

The History of Crime

Tombstone, Arizona

A silver strike launched Tombstone as a mining camp in 1879. By 1881 the town had 1,000 residents and a bloody reputation for violence. Two laws, passed in April, banned houses of prostitution and forbade carrying weapons inside the town's limits. Thus began a conflict that produced one of the Old West's most famous gunfights.

Sheriff John Behan, the top lawman in Cochise County, was a close friend of a local gang known as the Cowboys, rustlers and bandits led by the Clanton and McLaury brothers. Behan's primary rivals in politics and business were the three Earp brothers—Wyatt, Morgan and Virgil—who ran saloons and gambling halls with dentist-turned-gun-fighter John "Doc" Holliday. By mid-1881 Virgil Earp was Tombstone's town marshal and a deputy U.S. marshal, using his dual authority to investigate (some say harass) the Cowboys.

The feud boiled over on October 26, 1881, when Morgan Earp learned that five Cowboys had come to Tombstone wearing pistols. Backed by his brothers and Doc Holliday, Earp went to arrest them at the O.K. Corral. The dubious lawmen found five Cowboys—Ike and Billy Clanton, Frank and Tom McLaury, and Billy Claiborne—fully armed, in violation of the law. (Ike Clanton later claimed he had no weapons and did not participate in what came next.) Someone drew first, and when the shooting stopped a half-minute later, Billy Clanton and both McLaurys were dead, while Holliday, Morgan Earp, and Virgil Earp were wounded.

Sheriff Behan charged Doc Holliday and Wyatt Earp with murder, but a Tombstone grand jury refused to indict them. Unknown snipers wounded Virgil Earp in December 1881 and killed Morgan in March 1882. Wyatt then secured appointment as a deputy U.S. marshal and pursued the suspected killers, gunning down three more Cowboys before he and his brother, James, left Arizona in April 1882. John Behan lost his re-election bid in November 1882 but later served as deputy warden of Yuma Territorial Prison. Days after Behan's defeat, Billy Claiborne died in a Tombstone shootout with "Buckskin" Frank Leslie. Police killed Ike Clanton at Springville, Arizona, in June 1887.

The O.K. Corral gunfight spawned six Hollywood films between 1946 and 1994, plus an episode of *Star Trek* in October 1968, but it was only a minor skirmish in the long-running war against crime.

"THERE OUGHTA BE A LAW!"

Throughout recorded history, civilizations have sought to define and punish criminal behavior. The first known criminal laws were decreed by Urukagina, who ruled the Mesopotamian city-state of Lagash between 2380 and 2360 B.C. None of those documents survive today, but references in later works suggest that Urukagina's code was the first legal document to use the word *freedom* (*ama-gi* in Sumerian).[1]

The oldest known legal code still in existence, preserved on tablets dating from 2112 to 2095 B.C., is the Code of Ur-Nammu. Better preserved, and far better known, is the Code of Hammurabi, enacted by Babylon's king around 1760 B.C. Carved on a stone slab more than seven feet tall, the surviving portion of Hammurabi's code includes 282 separate laws governing various aspects of human behavior. The criminal code includes orders to execute those who "ensnare" others or falsely accuse their neighbors of crimes. Criminal charges were judged by having the suspect jump into a river. If he drowned, he was guilty, but if he survived, his accuser was slain.

Ancient Assyria, in western Asia, adopted similar codes around 1075 B.C., including rules that allowed a murder victim's relatives to execute the killer. Other laws prescribed amputation of fingers for various crimes, such as striking another man's wife and "meddling" with a neighbor's crops. Men who injured pregnant women, prostitutes who wore veils in public, and women who slapped men were punished by whipping. Death was the penalty for rape, adultery, and sorcery.

The Hebrew Bible (or Old Testament), compiled in ancient times and formally translated by Saint Jerome between 390 and 405, contains numerous laws of alleged divine origin. Most famous are the Ten Commandments of Exodus, restated and expanded in Deuteronomy, but many other laws also applied. Offenders could be executed for a list of crimes, including murder, kidnapping, striking or cursing one's parents, rebellion against parental or priestly authority, blasphemy or worship of "false" gods, violating the Sabbath, practicing magic or witchcraft, and various sexual offenses (including adultery, bestiality, homosexuality, incest, rape of an engaged or married woman, and premarital sex).

Ancient Roman law began with the Twelve Tables (449 B.C.) and expanded over the next thousand years to encompass an empire spanning the known world, from Ethiopia to Britain. Punishment for crime was harsh and often fatal, but royalty was generally exempt—at least, while holding power—and free to enjoy pastimes that might be considered outrageous today.

Muhammad (570–632) established the Muslim religion and laid down its earliest laws—called *sharia*—in the Koran, later amplified by successor Al-Shafi'i (767–820). While similar to the Hebrew Bible in many respects—with a near-identical ban on certain "unclean" foods— *sharia* also applied distinctly Islamic codes of conduct to all aspects of daily life, including business, family relationships, hygiene, and sexuality.

Britain's kings ruled by supposed "divine right," and their every word was law, until King John's defeat in battle by rebellious nobles forced him to accept the Magna Carta ("Great Charter") in 1215. That document limited royal powers and paved the way for development of "common law," based on the rulings of judges, rather than elected or appointed lawmakers. Still, punishments remained severe. King Henry VIII (1491–1547) executed an estimated 72,000 people between 1509 and 1547, many by torture. Prior to 1832, 220 different crimes were punished by death in Britain, including such offenses as "being in the company of Gypsies for one month" and "strong evidence of malice in a child aged 7–14 years of age."[2]

CODE OF UR-NAMMU

King Ur-Nammu of southern Mesopotamia assumed office in 2112 B.C. and ruled until his death in battle, 17 years later. His legal code, written around 2100 B.C., represents the oldest known system of formalized law on Earth. Fragments of the code were found and translated between 1952 and 1965, revealing 40 of an estimated 57 laws imposed by Ur-Nammu.

As with other ancient codes, certain crimes carried a death sentence under Ur-Nammu, including murder, robbery, and adultery. Accused sorcerers suffered trial by ordeal in water, but if they survived, their accusers were fined 33 grams of silver. A woman accused of adultery faced the same trial, and if found innocent received 330 grams of silver from her accuser. Other monetary fines were imposed for kidnapping (165 grams of silver), perjury (165 grams), rape of another man's female slave (66 grams), knocking out another person's eye (330 grams) or tooth (22 grams), cutting off another person's foot (110 grams) or nose (440 grams, provided that a copper knife was used), or crushing another's limb with a club (660 grams). A female slave who insulted her owners might have her mouth scoured with a quart of salt.[5]

Settlers in the present-day United States based their laws on statutes from their homelands and the Bible until 1787, when ratification of the U.S. Constitution made it the supreme law of the land. Individual states retained freedom to ban and punish specific activities, but the Constitution and its subsequent amendments established guidelines for criminal trials and guaranteed the right to legal counsel, while forbidding excessive bail, fines, or "cruel and unusual punishments."[3]

France followed America's lead and went further still, with enactment of a new Penal Code in 1791. Author Louis Michel Le Peletier de Saint-Fargeau (1760–93) sought to ban only "true crimes," not "phony offenses, created by superstition, feudalism, the tax system, and [royal] despotism." Thus, the new law eliminated penalties for religious offenses and same-sex liaisons.[4]

ENFORCING THE LAW

Passing laws is one thing; enforcing them is quite another. Each society establishes its own policing apparatus to solve crimes and punish offenders. Ancient Greece (1100–146 B.C.) used slaves as police. China began appointing "prefects" during the Chu kingdom (1030–223 B.C.) and later exported that system of law enforcement to Japan and Korea. The Roman Empire (27 B.C.–1453 A.D.) enforced its laws with troops abroad and watchmen called *vigiles* at home. After the Norman conquest of Britain (1066–69), local lords appointed constables ("counts of the stables") to keep the peace. Spain's unofficial *hermandad* ("brotherhood") enforced local laws from medieval times until 1835.

French King Louis XIV (1638–1715) created Europe's first formal police department to patrol Paris in March 1667, expanding that force to police the whole country in October 1699. Britain's first true law enforcement agency, the Thames River Police, was created in 1798 to suppress river piracy. Scotland's City of Glasgow Police soon followed in June 1800, surviving until 1975. Napoleon Bonaparte (1769–1821) expanded French police service in 1800, to include every city with more than 5,000 inhabitants.

In the United States, police work generally fell to constables or militia until 1838, when Boston established the country's first organized police force, followed by New York City (1844), New Orleans (1852), Philadelphia (1854), Chicago (1855), and Los Angeles (1869). Pennsylvania created the first state police force in 1902, in the aftermath of violent labor struggles. Federal policing dates from President George Washington's appointment of the first U.S. Marshals in 1789, through creation of the Secret Service in 1865 and the FBI's establishment in 1908, with steady expansion of federal authority over the past century.

Law enforcement in the Old West often fell to rough men who themselves resembled outlaws. The Earp brothers ran brothels in Dodge City, Kansas, during the late 1870s, where locals dubbed them "the fighting pimps." Dallas Stoudenmire (1845–82) served as a Texas Ranger and a deputy U.S. Marshal, while engaging in numerous drunken gunfights. During service as sheriff of Abilene, Kansas, James "Wild Bill" Hickok (1837–76) accidentally killed his own deputy. Arizona sheriff Burt

Alvord (1866-1910) stole cattle in his spare time and received a two-year prison term in 1904.[6]

Modern police departments operate within specific jurisdictions (areas of authority) defined by law. State and local police are confined by political boundaries, while various special departments protect a particular park, public building, or industry. Other agencies investigate only specific types of crime: drug offenses, tax evasion, arson, computer crimes, and so on.

In the United States, most crimes were state or local problems until the 20th century, when gradual expansion of the federal government imposed new laws from coast to coast. Most federal laws are based upon the Constitution's "commerce clause" (Article 1, Section 8, Clause 3), which grants Congress sole power to regulate trade between states or between the United States and foreign countries. Over the past 100 years, that clause has justified various laws involving crimes that cross state lines.

Federal expansion began with the Mann Act of 1910, punishing interstate transport of women for "immoral purposes," and continued with the Dyer Act of 1919, which outlawed driving stolen cars across state lines. The Volstead Act of 1920 banned liquor nationwide until its repeal in 1933. America's first "crime war," in 1932–34, produced new laws punishing interstate kidnapping, robbery of federally insured banks, and flight across state lines to escape prosecution or incarceration. Possession of specific "gangster weapons" was also restricted (but not banned) in 1934, paving the way for future gun-control statutes. The first of many federal drug laws, the Marijuana Tax Act, passed Congress in 1937. Wire fraud—using the telephone or telegraph to steal—was banned in 1948, later expanded to include television and computers. Modern civil rights laws date from 1957. The first federal laws addressing organized crime were not passed until 1970. The same year witnessed passage of the Federal Explosives Law, designed to punish bombers.

KEEPING UP WITH CRIME

Law enforcement is generally reactive, responding to crimes as they happen, and criminals often adopt new technology before police decide (or can afford) to update methods and equipment. No one can predict the impact of a new drug, weapon, vehicle, or software program on society until its use in crime reveals the need for new techniques to curb the trend.

Early police patrolled their routes on foot, using horses for crowd control or to chase mounted outlaws. Some departments still use hors-

THE RICO ACT

Organized crime has plagued American society since Prohibition turned small-time local gangsters into millionaires with international influence, but efforts to restrict it were haphazard prior to October 15, 1970, when Congress passed the Organized Crime Control Act. That statute imposed federal penalties for any illegal gambling operation involving five or more persons, which continues for more than 30 days or earns $2,000 in a single day. The law also includes another statute, called the Racketeer Influenced and Corrupt Organizations (RICO) Act, written to define and punish crimes long known as "racketeering."

While the term *racket* was first applied to criminal activity in 1591, and to organized gangsters in 1928, definitions varied widely until 1970.[7] The new law listed 35 specific crimes—27 federal and eight state offenses—and specified that any group of people who committed two or more within a 10-year period may be convicted of racketeering. The specific crimes include bribery, counterfeiting, embezzlement, various frauds, gambling, theft, money laundering, trafficking in drugs or obscene material, transporting illegal aliens for profit, murder-for-hire, and terrorism. Conviction carries a sentence of 25 years and a $25,000 fine on each count, plus forfeiture of any cash or property obtained through racketeering.

Robert Blakey, author of the RICO Act, desired wide application of the law, stating: "We don't want one set of rules for people whose collars are blue or whose names end in vowels, and another set for those whose collars are white and have Ivy League diplomas."[8] Famous RICO targets include:

es—the U.S. Border Patrol had 205 horses in 2005[9]—but police lagged behind criminals in adopting modern vehicles. British police in Kent bought 20 bicycles in 1896, and 129 rural departments had bike patrols by 1904.[10] The first police "car" was an electric street wagon, launched in Akron, Ohio, in 1899. Its top speed was 16 miles per hour, and its battery needed recharging every 30 miles.[11] Police motorcycles first

- The Hells Angels Motorcycle Club, whose president and several members were charged in 1979 with trafficking in drugs and weapons. Jurors failed to reach a verdict, saying that prosecutors did not prove the crimes reflected club policy.
- Florida's Key West Police Department, declared a "criminal enterprise" after several top officers were charged with aiding cocaine smugglers in June 1984.
- Michael Milken, a stock swindler indicted on 98 counts in March 1989. He pled guilty on six reduced charges to avoid a life prison term, received 10 years, and was paroled in less than two.
- The Pro-Life Action Network, antiabortion crusaders sued on RICO charges in 1989, for obstructing clinic entrances. In 1998 federal jurors found the defendants responsible for acts of violence and intimidation, resulting in a nationwide injunction against "pro-life" terrorism. In 2003 the U.S. Supreme Court reversed that verdict, finding that RICO violations must have a financial motive.
- Mohawk Industries of Georgia, accused in 2004 of hiring illegal aliens. An appellate court upheld the lawsuit in 2006, and the U.S. Supreme Court declined to review it in 2007. Trial remains pending.
- New York City's Gambino Mafia "family," four of whose leaders received life prison terms for RICO violations in October 2006.

Some sources claim that Robert Blakey named his law specifically so that its initials would spell "RICO," a reference to the name of a gangster portrayed by actor Edward G. Robinson in the 1931 film *Little Caesar.* Blakey has never confirmed or denied that assertion.[12]

A Border Patrol officer finishes getting his horse ready for the day's work. *AP Photo/John Miller*

appeared in Detroit and Evanston, Illinois, in 1908, while the Berkeley (California) Police Department established the first official motorcycle patrol three years later. New York City created the first police aviation department in 1919, with purchase of the two airplanes. Chicago police instituted "motor patrols" in 1921, and New York had dozens of police cars on the streets two years later.

Communication is vital for effective police work. Albany, New York, pioneered telegraph service for police and firefighters in 1877, while 1878 saw the first telephones installed at police stations in Washington, D.C. Detroit's police inaugurated use of one-way radio alerts in 1923, while Chicago's force experimented with "wireless telephone" systems. Australia introduced the first two-way police radios in 1923, but America stalled until 1933, when Bayonne, New Jersey, adopted the system.

Scientific crime fighting dominates modern prime-time television, but it had a slow start among real-world police. Frenchman Edmund Locard established the first crime laboratory in 1910, but the Los Angeles Police Department (LAPD) waited 13 more years to create America's first forensic lab, and the world famous FBI Laboratory did not open until November 1932. British physician Nehemiah Grew (1641–1712) published the first study of human fingerprints in 1684, but the first police use of fingerprint evidence did not occur until 1892 in Argentina. American police only began fingerpinting criminals in 1906.

The same delay is seen in other scientific fields. The first radar device was patented in 1904, but police only discovered its value for traffic enforcement in 1948. Computers as we know them date from 1941, but the first police application (in New Orleans) waited until 1955. Another decade passed before St. Louis pioneered computer-dispatched patrol cars, and most American departments still had no computers when the FBI National Crime Information Center went online in 1967. Alabama passed the first law governing computer crimes in 1975, but Congress did not follow suit until 1986, with passage of the Computer Fraud and Abuse Act.

Law enforcement is dangerous business, yet police have been slow to adopt new weapons. Texas Rangers replaced their single-shot pistols with Colt revolvers in 1847, but when criminals made the leap to machine guns and semiautomatic weapons in the 1920s, many police

A police officer holds a taser gun used to subdue suspected criminals. The gun can also be used as a stun gun, as demonstrated by the electricity arcing across its front. *AP Photo/Bob Child*

departments were reluctant to do likewise. FBI agents carried .38-caliber revolvers until 1986, when a bloody shootout in Miami left two agents dead and five wounded by bandits armed with automatic rifles. Italian inventor Filippo Negroli created the first "bulletproof vest" in 1538, but most American police shunned body armor until the 1930s, and lightweight Kevlar vests did not enter general use until 1972.

Urban riots in the 1960s spurred developments of nonlethal weapons and crowd-control agents. Tear gas, first introduced by French troops in World War I (1914-18), had limited effectiveness in open areas, prompting the invention of "Chemical Mace" in 1962 and stronger "pepper spray" in 1982. Other nonlethal weapons—some of which may still be fatal if improperly applied—include electric stun guns, riot foam that renders streets too slick for walking, and bullets made from rubber, plastic, wax, or wood to stun without causing permanent harm.

Whatever mission and methods are used, the task of crime fighting falls to human beings who accept the risks inherent in their work.

3

Local Police

New Orleans, Louisiana

Officer Nicola Cotton was alone in her patrol car at 10:00 A.M. on January 28, 2008, when she spotted Bernel Johnson in a parking lot on Earhart Boulevard. Johnson, age 44, matched the description of an unknown suspect in a recent sexual assault. Officer Cotton stopped to question him, and Johnson's gruff, evasive answers deepened her suspicion. As she prepared to handcuff Johnson, he pulled away and lashed out with his fists.

Officer Cotton struggled to defend herself against the violent suspect who was twice her size, but it proved to be a losing fight. First, Johnson wrenched a two-way radio from Cotton's hands, then seized her baton and struck her a stunning blow to the head. Still not satisfied, Johnson snatched Cotton's automatic pistol from her holster and shot her 15 times at close range. A two-year veteran of the New Orleans Police Department, Officer Cotton was 24 years old and eight weeks pregnant when she died.

Backup arrived minutes too late, but responding officers found Johnson hiding nearby, still clutching Officer Cotton's empty pistol. After he was booked on murder charges, held without bail, police learned that Johnson had been detained for psychiatric observation on January 4 for causing a disturbance at a local bank. Before that, he was expelled from a Salvation Army homeless shelter for attacking another resident with a fork. The latest charge seemed likely to ensure that he would never walk

The funeral procession of slain New Orleans police officer, Nicola Cotton, proceeds to the cemetery in New Orleans. Cotton was shot and killed while trying to arrest suspect Bernel Johnson. *AP Photo/ Bill Haber*

the streets again, but it came too late for Officer Cotton—the 108th New Orleans police officer killed on duty since 1856.[1]

STANDING WATCH

People often take local police for granted, but they did not always exist in their present form. America's first British colonists arrived at Jamestown, Virginia, in 1607, and while they quickly began writing laws, no organized means of enforcement existed for another quarter-century. Boston established the first formal night watch in 1631, followed by

Jamestown and New Amsterdam (now New York) in 1658, but citizens were left to defend themselves during daylight hours.

The U.S. Constitution, ratified in 1788, defined the powers and duties of America's federal government, but it left most law enforcement problems to the states. Throughout the country's founding era (1783–1815), civilian militias dealt with major problems, such as riots and disasters, and left city dwellers to cope with their local offenders. Some towns appointed constables, while others called their watchmen *marshals* (from the Old High German term for "stable keeper"). Both titles still remain in use for certain local law enforcement officers today.

The early constables and marshals generally worked part time, without badges, uniforms, or pay, earning small fees for serving writs and warrants. They received no special training and supplied their own weapons, if any were required. As America expanded westward, so did crime. Most towns of any significant size hired marshals to deal with rowdies and outlaws. As in the East, training was nonexistent, but lawmen were commonly known for their skill with firearms, learned as soldiers, Indian fighters, or even as criminals.

And they were all men in those days. America's first policewoman would not be hired until 1910, when the Los Angeles Police Department (LAPD) assigned social worker Alice Stebbins Wells (1873–1957) to patrol public facilities frequented by women and children, such as dance halls, movie theaters, and skating rinks. Wells remained on the job until 1940, by which time the LAPD had 38 more female officers assigned to duties, including criminal investigations.[2] In the Old West, meanwhile, it would be characters such as the Earps, Wild Bill Hickock, and Bat Masterson who brawled and shot their way into folklore.

While Hollywood has greatly exaggerated the Wild West's history of violence, law enforcement on the frontier was dangerous, as it remains today. A case in point is that of William Bailey, hired as a special officer to keep the peace during an August 1871 election in Newton, Kansas. Ironically, Bailey quarreled over politics with another policeman, Mike McCluskie, on August 11 and died when McCluskie shot him twice in the chest. McCluskie fled town, but later returned to plead self-defense (though Bailey had not drawn a gun). On the night of August 19, a group of Bailey's friends found McCluskie playing cards at a local saloon. Insults led to shooting, which left McCluskie and three others dead, with four men wounded. The so-called Newton Massacre was thus a bloodier engagement than Arizona's O.K. Corral gunfight, 10 years later, but the absence of famous shooters leaves it almost forgotten today.

HIGH CRIMES AND MISDEMEANORS

Modern America has 4,710 municipal law enforcement agencies operating from coast to coast.[3] Their jurisdiction is defined by the physical boundaries of the city or town they serve and by the kinds of laws which they enforce. Those fall into three categories:

Local ordinances, imposing penalties for certain acts within the city limits. Ordinances cover a broad range of topics, including traffic and parking, curfews, public nuisances, commercial regulations, and so on. Violation of a local ordinance is usually called an infraction or violation, rather than a crime. Punishment generally involves a monetary fine or short term in the local jail. Many jurisdictions try such cases before a local magistrate or justice of the peace, without a jury.

Misdemeanors, next up the punishment scale, with a maximum sentence of one year or less in jail. Most cases are settled with fines, unless repeat offenders or some violent behavior is involved. State lawmakers create misdemeanor statutes, but local police enforce them within their specific jurisdictions.

Felonies, the most serious crimes, for which prison terms exceed one year and may include the death penalty. As with misdemeanors, felony statutes are passed by state or federal legislators, but enforcement (in the case of state crimes) falls to local police in most cases. Felons are the criminals most likely to engage in violence, although police report that traffic violations and family quarrels produce many assaults upon officers handling "routine" duties.

1. Local police departments are normally established along paramilitary lines, with ranks, uniforms, and insignia denoting levels of authority or special assignments. Depending on the locale, a department's leader may be called the chief, constable, or marshal, with some known by a rank (such as "colonel") established in the department's charter. Lower ranks commonly bear such

titles as captain, lieutenant, sergeant, inspector, and detective. The lowest-ranking members are generally known simply as officers, patrolmen, or deputies, and sometimes as privates.

2. Most local police chiefs are hired by the town's mayor or council, but city marshals are elected in Missouri as a town's chief law enforcement officer. In Colorado, residents of different towns choose between electing a marshal or leaving city leaders to hire a chief of police. In New York, city marshals are elected to serve specific towns, except for New York City, where the mayor appoints 83 marshals to unpaid positions involving collection of legal judgments, enforcing court orders, and performing evictions. In Ohio, village marshals perform the same functions, serving directly under a mayor. Texas city marshals and their deputies serve towns that cannot afford a full police force.

HEROES OF 9/11

On the morning of September 11, 2001, terrorists hijacked four commercial airliners for use as flying bombs against selected targets in the eastern United States. Two of the planes crashed into the twin towers of New York's World Trade Center at 8:46 and 9:03 A.M., causing the south tower to collapse at 9:59, followed by the north tower at 10:28. During the 102 minutes between first impact and final collapse, New York police, firefighters and paramedics worked nonstop to rescue survivors from the burning towers.

And 403 of them died in the process.

The final death toll at ground zero was 2,819. That tally included 23 NYPD officers and 37 Port Authority police, plus 343 firefighters and paramedics. Also lost at the scene were five agents from the New York State Department of Taxation and Finance, three officers from the New York State Office of Court Administration, one New York City fire marshal, and one FBI agent.[4]

As tragic as those losses were, the suffering did not end on 9/11. Exposure to toxic dust and fumes released by the

3. While municipal police may serve a town of any size, the term *metropolitan police* applies to major cities and surrounding areas. Examples include the St. Louis (Missouri) Metropolitan Police Department, created in 1861; the Las Vegas (Nevada) Metropolitan Police Department, formed in 1973 by a merger of city police with the Clark County Sheriff's Department; the Miami-Dade County Police Department, created by merging city police with the Dade County Sheriff's Department in 1981; and the Indianapolis Metropolitan Police Department, created by merging city police with the Marion County Sheriff's Department in 2007.

COUNTY AGENCIES

In America, the next level of government above municipalities is known as a county in 48 states, as a borough in Alaska, and as a parish

explosions and fires at the World Trade Center scarred the lungs of many other rescue workers, leaving them susceptible to cancer and other deadly diseases. Dr. Stephen Levin, director of the World Trade Center Worker and Volunteer Medical Screening Program, told reporters in 2006, "We have thousands of people who were down there with unprotected exposures. Many will develop asthma and a few will develop this terrible lung scarring that leads to disability or death." The final toll, by Levin's estimation, may exceed 7,200 victims.[5]

Strangely, NYPD's Police Bureau has resisted acknowledging injuries caused by inhaling toxic particles, insisting that contamination from the site had no link to the death of at least two policemen. Officer James Godbee developed a steadily worsening cough during 850 hours of work at ground zero, leading to collapse of one lung in March 2004 and his death nine months later. Another NYPD officer, James Zadroga, died from a similar ailment in January 2006. In both cases—and many others thus far without fatal results—police administrators deny any link to the 9/11 tragedy. Meanwhile, leaders of the New York Fire Department publicly acknowledge the connection with regard to ailing firefighters.

RODNEY KING

On the night of March 3, 1991, a California Highway Patrol officer observed an African-American motorist with two passengers, driving at dangerous speeds through Los Angeles. LAPD units joined the chase as driver Rodney King—intoxicated and afraid of being jailed for violating parole on a robbery conviction—tried to evade the officers. When King finally stopped, his passengers surrendered and were quickly handcuffed. King appeared aggressive and disoriented—giggling, shouting, and waving at helicopters overhead. When he advanced toward LAPD Officer Laurence Powell, Powell struck King with his baton.

What happened next remains a subject of heated controversy. Unnoticed by police, bystander George Holliday videotaped Officers Powell, Timothy Wind, and Theodore Briseno repeatedly clubbing and kicking King, apparently directed by Sergeant Stacey Koon. When finally transported to a hospital, King tested negative for illegal drugs, but his blood-alcohol level registered twice the legal limit.

L.A.'s district attorney charged Briseno, Koon, Powell, and Wind with using excessive force. Their trial was held in Simi Valley, a mostly white suburb where many LAPD officers

in Louisiana. Each county has its own elected government and law enforcement agencies—a total of 2,409 nationwide, at the time of this writing.[6] Counties contain various towns and cities, but county police generally avoid pursuit of criminals inside a city's recognized limits, unless they are invited to participate or crimes occur on county-owned property, such as a courthouse, fairgrounds, or park. Towns with limited budgets may also hire county officers to provide police service, in lieu of creating their own departments. Hawaii is unique in having only county law enforcement agencies, with no city police.

In most states a county's chief law enforcement officer is known as the sheriff, a term derived from the British "shire reeve," a county office created in 1252 that combined the duties of a watchman with other reside. On April 29, 1992, jurors convicted Laurence Powell but acquitted the other defendants. Mayor Tom Bradley, himself an African American, told reporters, "The jury's verdict will not blind us to what we saw on that videotape. The men who beat Rodney King do not deserve to wear the uniform of the LAPD."[7] News of the officers' acquittal sparked rioting in L.A.'s black neighborhoods, where 53 persons died and 2,383 were injured, while 7,000 fires caused an estimated $1 billion in damage. Smaller riots occurred in other cities nationwide, including Atlanta, Georgia, and Las Vegas, Nevada.[8]

The officers who beat King faced a second trial in federal court, in February 1993. This time, jurors convicted Sgt. Koon and Officer Powell of violating King's civil rights, while Officers Briseno and Wind were acquitted. King sued the city of Los Angeles and won $3.8 million, which he used to start a hip-hop music label. In May 1991 he was jailed for trying to run a policeman down with his car, receiving a 90-day sentence. In August 2003 another drunken high-speed chase left King with a fractured pelvis, after his car crashed into a house. In November 2007 he was shot by thieves who stole his bicycle, but managed to survive his wounds. In October 2008 he appeared on TV's reality program *Celebrity Rehab with Dr. Drew.*

political and ceremonial tasks. Most county sheriffs are elected, and while many in the not-so-distant past had no experience or training in police work, most modern states and counties require candidates for sheriff to meet professional standards established by law. Hawaii is again unique, calling its state police the State of Hawaii Sheriff's Office.

Traditionally, county sheriffs and their deputies perform a wider range of duties than those carried out by municipal police. Aside from serving as a county's top law enforcement officer with full police powers, most sheriffs also manage and maintain their county's jails, provide security as bailiffs in county courts, serve court documents (including subpoenas, summonses, warrants, and writs), and enforce monetary decrees from the court (such as child support payments, wage

A fire burns out of control in the South Central section of Los
Angeles on April 30, 1992. Hundreds of stores were burned when
rioting erupted after the verdicts in the Rodney King assault
case. *AP Photo/Paul Sakuma*

garnishment, and sale of foreclosed property at auction). Some sheriffs
also serve as their county's tax collectors, but the potential for abuse and
corruption in that area has prompted most counties to elect separate
treasurers or tax assessors. In a few jurisdictions, sheriffs also double
as coroners, the officers responsible for determining causes of death.
Again, since few (if any) sheriffs are medically qualified as pathologists,
many counties employ a trained medical examiner or use state facilities
for cause-of-death investigations.

The relationship between county and municipal police is sometimes
strained. Few cases reach the extremes seen in Tombstone, Arizona,
during 1881, but turf wars and tension may hamper effective law

enforcement. In Selma, Alabama, during 1965, Police Chief Wilson Baker opposed Sheriff Jim Clark's policy of beating and jailing African-American civil rights demonstrators, with the result that the men became bitter enemies. Longstanding rivalry between the LAPD and the Los Angeles County Sheriff's Department was even more notorious. Each side accused the other of mishandling crucial evidence in the "Manson Family" murders of 1969, and L.A.'s FBI office maintained two separate teams to investigate bank robberies, one working with LAPD, the other with the sheriff's office. FBI Director J. Edgar Hoover aggravated that feud in the 1960s, supporting the county sheriff while waging a personal vendetta against LAPD Chief William Parker, whom Hoover personally despised.[9]

State Police

Arkville, New York

On April 24, 2007, New York State Trooper Matthew Gombosi stopped the driver of a Dodge minivan for speeding through tiny Margaretville, a village with fewer than 700 residents. Gombosi did not know the vehicle was stolen, but when driver Travis Trim failed to present proper identification, Gombosi ordered him out of the van, prepared to arrest Trim for driving without a license. Instead of complying, Trim drew a pistol and shot Gombosi in the chest. A Kevlar vest saved Gombosi's life, but he still lay stunned as the van sped away.

Alerted to the shooting, officers swarmed over Delaware County's back roads, seeking the still-unidentified gunman. They soon found his van abandoned in nearby Middletown, then focused on a farmhouse outside Arkville (population 893) when its burglar alarm alerted manhunters to an intruder. Trooper David Brinkerhoff was first on the scene, closely followed by six members of the New York State Police Mobile Response Team. Searching the house, they found Trim on the second floor. Trim shot Brinkerhoff, but again Kevlar foiled his intent to kill. An intense exchange of gunfire followed, during which Trim wounded a second trooper, while a third accidentally shot and killed Brinkerhoff.

Retreating with their wounded, the officers waited for reinforcements. After a four-hour standoff, police fired tear gas into the farmhouse, which soon burst into flames. Unable to control the fire, officers

44

Members of the New York State Police Mobile Response Team rush a farmhouse in Arkville, New York, on April 25, 2007. Trooper David Brinkerhoff, a member of the Mobile Response Team, was killed in a shootout in the house earlier that day. *AP Photo/Mike Groll, File*

watched the house burn down then combed the ashes. They found Trim's corpse in the ruins, reportedly killed by a gunshot before the fire reached him. Trooper Brinkerhoff was the 115th New York State Police officer killed in the line of duty since 1920.[1]

STATES' RIGHTS AND WRONGS

According to the U.S. Constitution's Tenth Amendment, any "powers not delegated to the United States by the Constitution, nor prohibited by it to the States, are reserved to the States respectively, or to the people." In 1788 that meant each state was responsible for defining and punishing most crimes within its borders, as well as establishing guidelines for education, marriage, voting (except in federal elections), and a wide range of other topics. Over the next 221 years, states' rights would remain a heated subject of debate, as federal authority expanded and the states were forced to yield.

Almost from the beginning, various state leaders balked at paying taxes and providing troops for federal duty. The argument reached its peak in 1860, when congressional opposition to slavery drove 11 southern states to leave the Union and form a rival nation of their own. The Civil War settled that argument in 1865, but another hundred years would pass before 42 states on both sides of the Mason-Dixon Line surrendered their "right" to segregate or otherwise discriminate against racial minorities. More recent disputes between Washington and various states include restrictions placed on use of federal land, environmental protection measures opposed by local industries, dumping of toxic waste, and petroleum drilling in national parks. Some states and cities also claim that Washington exerts too much authority in second-guessing criminal procedures.

Even with their grant of constitutional authority, state governments were slow to accept responsibility for law enforcement. Pennsylvania built the country's first state prison in 1790, but another 21 years passed before another state—Georgia—followed that example. County jails housed most prisoners into the mid-19th century, and sheriffs executed condemned inmates until 1834, when Pennsylvania bucked the trend by moving its gallows to Eastern State Penitentiary.

America's earliest state police were called rangers ("wanderers" or "rovers"), a term first applied to British gamekeepers in the 14th century. First came the Texas Rangers, established in 1823 and formally organized in 1835, then the California Rangers, founded in 1854. In both cases, the units devoted much of their time to battling Indian tribes rather than pursuing outlaws. Massachusetts created the first true statewide police force in 1865, though it remained small and loosely organized until 1921. California disbanded its rangers in 1887, and for the next 42 years confined state officers to guarding the capitol building in Sacramento. Arizona created a ranger force in 1901, but scrapped it in 1909. Other early state police departments included those organized in Connecticut (1903), New Mexico (1905), Pennsylvania (1905), and Nevada (1908).

Eastern State Penitentiary in Philadelphia, built in 1790, was the first state prison built in the United States. *AP Photo/Matt Rourke*

THE NEW BREED

As usual, development of modern state police forces required emergencies to justify the move—and the expense—of training and equipping officers for statewide duty. In the 20th century, those circumstances included Prohibition, widespread labor strikes accompanied by violence, and mass production of automobiles.

Many states were already "dry" when the Constitution's Eighteenth Amendment banned alcoholic beverages nationwide in 1920, but Americans kept drinking in thousands of illegal saloons, supplied by smugglers who formed the first national crime syndicate during 1927–29. With only 1,520 federal agents assigned to patrol the whole country, states shouldered much of the enforcement burden. Meanwhile, the price of Henry Ford's Model-T roadster dropped from $850 in 1909 to $300 in the 1920s, putting legions of new drivers on the road. Accidents and auto thefts proliferated. Bank robbers and other criminals enjoyed mobility that most police departments lacked.

The answer seemed to be creation of new state police agencies, though early duties varied. Some states called their new teams highway patrols, to emphasize traffic safety enforcement, while leaving criminal

FRANK HAMER (1884–1955)

The Texas Rangers hold near-legendary status in American history, ranking as the oldest state police department, with their adventures dramatized in novels since 1856, in at least a dozen feature films since 1936, on radio during the 1950s, and in various television series from 1965 to 2005. And still, after 186 years, no other single Ranger rivals Frank Hamer's claim to fame.

Born in 1884 at Fairview, Texas, Hamer fought his first gun battle at age 16, with a farmer who tried to hire him as a contract killer. Though wounded, Hamer survived that fight; his opponent did not. Hamer joined the Rangers in 1906, then left to serve as Navasota's town marshal from 1908 to 1911, but rejoined the Rangers in 1915. By the time he finally retired, in 1949, Hamer had fought more than 100 gunfights, killing 53 outlaws, while suffering 17 gunshot and stab wounds.[2]

Of all the outlaws tracked by Hamer, none was more famous than lethal lovers Clyde Barrow (1909–34) and Bonnie Parker (1910–34). With other members of their gang, Clyde and Bonnie killed at least 12 victims, most of them lawmen, between 1930 and 1934. Hamer was assigned to hunt them down after the gang staged a Texas prison break in January 1934, slaying one guard and wounding another. Hamer stalked the gang from February 1 until May 23, 1934, when his posse ambushed the couple in Louisiana, riddling them with bullets before they could reach their weapons.

Hamer died peacefully in his sleep on July 10, 1955. Twelve years later, the Hollywood film *Bonnie and Clyde* portrayed him as a vindictive figure, stalking the Barrow gang because they had captured and embarrassed him—an event that never happened in real life. Texans remember Hamer as a rugged officer who never flinched from danger, and who always got his man—dead or alive.

investigations to county sheriffs and city police. Other states invested their officers—sometimes called state troopers, initially a term for mounted cavalry—with full police powers.

Michigan and New York led the way with state police forces created in 1917. Idaho and West Virginia followed suit in 1919. The Roaring Twenties saw new state police forces launched in Maryland, Maine, New Jersey, and Washington (1921); Illinois and Louisiana (1922); Delaware and Utah (1923); Rhode Island (1925); Georgia (1927); and California, Minnesota, North Carolina, and Tennessee (1929).

While Prohibition continued through 1933, the Wall Street crash of 1929 plunged America into its Great Depression, leaving millions out of work and homeless. People wandered from coast to coast in search of jobs, relief programs, and warmer climates. This mass migration of the poor encouraged creation of new state police forces to stem the tide. Those newly created included South Carolina (1930); Missouri and Oregon (1931); Virginia (1932); Indiana, Ohio, and Wyoming (1933); Alabama, Arkansas, Colorado, Iowa, Montana, North Dakota, and South Dakota (1935); Kansas, Nebraska, New Hampshire, and Oklahoma (1937); Mississippi (1938); and Florida and Wisconsin (1939).

Crime rates declined during World War II, as jobs proliferated and many Americans entered military service. War demands also reduced production of civilian automobiles and rationed gasoline purchases, which eased the burden of state traffic enforcement during 1941-45. Alaska's highway patrol, formed in 1941, was the only new state police agency created during the war. Restoration of peace brought the usual rise in crime nationwide, coupled with a new surge in auto sales, prompting creation of state police forces in Vermont (1947) and Kentucky (1948). In 1953, six years before achieving statehood, Alaska lawmakers transformed their highway patrol into a full-service territorial police force.

WHAT'S IN A NAME?

At the time of this writing, the 50 states maintained 362 agencies to enforce various aspects of state law. Twenty-five states refer to their state police by that name or some variant (state patrol or state troopers). Nine states invest their highway patrol agencies with full police powers. Hawaii calls its state police the State of Hawaii Sheriff's Office. Ten states maintain both a highway patrol and a separate force to investigate crimes. Of those, five states refer to the criminal branch as a "bureau of investigation," borrowing that name from the more famous FBI. In 30 of the 50 states, a Department of Public Safety supervises state police activities, while providing other services related to law enforcement.[3]

State police duties are not limited to traffic patrols and generic criminal investigations. Every state has a department of corrections or some equivalent organization, which maintains and supervises state prisons. Eighteen states have specific agencies assigned to regulate production and sale of alcoholic beverages, and five support units designed to suppress illegal drug traffic. Twenty-two states and the District of Columbia have special police departments assigned to protect capitol buildings, and four have additional teams to guard public officials, patterned after the U.S. Secret Service. Seventeen states have fire marshals or equivalent officers on standby to investigate arson cases. Nationwide, 64 different state agencies monitor environmental violations related to wildlife and pollution, while 21 others exist specifically to patrol state parks. Fifteen agencies in 13 states police coastal waters, docks, and rivers. Fourteen states have agencies assigned to supervise commercial vehicles, six others police public transportation in various forms, and two states (Connecticut and Maryland) have police forces assigned to airports. Seven states have agencies created to supervise licensed gambling, six support university police departments, and five maintain units to police mental hospitals. Six states have agencies assigned full time to fraud investigations.[4]

Often overlooked when state police groups are considered, various other specialized agencies operate with little or no public recognition. Some of those units include:

- The Georgia World Congress Center Department of Public Safety, created in 1995 to protect Atlanta's Congress Center, the Georgia Dome, and Centennial Olympic Park. Its 30 officers patrol on foot, on bicycles, and in automobiles.
- The Kentucky Horse Park Police, organized to patrol Lexington's Kentucky Horse Park, a 1,200-acre theme park and retirement

home for celebrated racehorses, opened in 1978 to celebrate "man's relationship with the horse."

o The Commonwealth of Pennsylvania Bureau of Dog Law Enforcement, created to inspect commercial kennels statewide.

o Louisiana's Livestock Brand Commission, founded to investigate agricultural crimes, including thefts of livestock, farm machinery, and equipment. LBC agents also record livestock brands and publish them in book form at five-year intervals, collect livestock statistics in collaboration with the U.S. Department of Agriculture, and control "nuisance animals" deemed detrimental to farms or forests.

o The Levee District Police, assigned to patrol Louisiana's inland waterways, in pursuit of offenders ranging from poachers and smugglers to saboteurs and terrorists.

o New Jersey's Election Law Enforcement Commission, created in 1973 to investigate violations of state campaign-finance laws.

o The North Carolina Museum of Art Special Police, organized to protect Raleigh's premier museum and the surrounding 164 acres of Museum Park, established in the 1940s.

SERVANTS OF THE STATE

State police enforce the same misdemeanor and felony statutes enforced by local authorities, and while their jurisdiction technically covers all parts of the state (except land owned by the federal government), state police jurisdiction is commonly limited by custom or by law. Traffic enforcement provides a case in point, where municipal police patrol city streets, county officers monitor roads built and maintained with county funds, and state police pursue violators on state and U.S. highways. (There is no federal highway patrol.) In criminal cases, state police generally leave investigations to local officers unless a crime occurs on state property or local agencies request assistance. State police or highway patrolmen are also frequently mobilized to deal with large-scale riots and natural disasters.

The functions of state police are defined by law, but in practical terms their deployment is often influenced by politics. Pennsylvania's state police were organized as a direct result of violence surrounding strikes by coal miners, but when new strikes occurred in 1910–11, many witnesses accused the troopers of unprovoked beatings and shootings, as well as sexual assaults on miners' wives.[5] State police throughout the country faced similar accusations of strikebreaking during the 1920s and 1930s, when violence was common on both sides and politicians who controlled the state police were often friendly with industrial leaders who opposed labor unions.

The long campaign for African-American civil rights revealed both strengths and weaknesses in southern state police. When Ku Klux Klan (KKK) members attacked integrated "freedom riders" in May 1961, Alabama Highway Patrol officer E. L. Cowling single-handedly prevented the mob from storming one bus and mauling its passengers. A month later, Governor John Patterson threatened to fire any state officer who spoke to FBI agents investigating civil rights complaints. In 1962 Alabama voters elected Governor George Wallace (1919–98) on his promise to maintain "segregation forever." Wallace named Albert Lingo (1910–69), a "good friend" of the KKK, to serve as Alabama's Public Safety Director. Lingo turned the highway patrol into a strike force against civil rights demonstrators, decorated patrol cars and uniforms with Confederate flags, and conspired with Klan members to conceal evidence of terrorist bombings. When Wallace sought re-election in 1970, he frightened white voters with claims that his opponent would integrate the highway patrol, implying that black officers might harass or molest white women.[6]

The Mississippi Highway Patrol suffered similar problems in the 1960s. Some officers participated in a riot against integration of the state university in September 1962, and FBI agents identified several highway patrolmen as active members of the KKK, linking them to harassment and beatings of civil rights workers. Other officers performed their duties conscientiously and showed great courage, considering the climate of the times. In 1964 they obtained a confession from Klansman James Seale, who had murdered two black teenagers and was suspected in the beating death of a fellow Klan member who opposed acts of violence. Despite Seale's admission, white prosecutors refused to place him on trial for his crimes. Seale was finally convicted on federal kidnapping and conspiracy charges in August 2007, receiving a life sentence, but an appellate court overturned that

New York State Police patrol the grounds of Attica prison after the September 1971 riot. *AP Photo*

verdict in September 2008, noting that the statute of limitations had expired.[7]

New York State Police were drawn into a deadly confrontation on September 9, 1971, after 1,000 prisoners rebelled against their jailers at the Attica Correctional Facility, seizing 33 guards as hostages. When negotiations failed to resolve the standoff, Governor Nelson Rockefeller (1908–79) ordered state police to retake the prison. According to a report from the New York State Special Commission on Attica, "With the exception of Indian massacres in the late 19th century, the State Police assault which ended the four-day prison uprising was the bloodiest one-day encounter between Americans since the Civil War." Specifically, state troopers tear-gassed the prison yard at 9:46 A.M. on September 13, then fired rifles and shotguns into the clouds of gas for two full minutes, killing 28 inmates and nine of the 33 hostages. (Reports that the guards were slain and mutilated by inmates proved to be false.) Afterward, prison doctors reported that troopers and guards severely beat many inmates, including some who were not involved in the riot.[8]

ATTACK ON TERROR

In post-9/11 America, most state police agencies created new divisions to collaborate with the FBI and the U.S. Department of Homeland Security in collecting evidence of potential terrorist threats. Colonel Thomas Foley, head of the Massachusetts State Police, announced his agency's shift in priorities on December 13, 2001, and other departments soon followed, energized by the attacks that claimed thousands of lives. Some 1,200 persons were jailed nationwide as alleged "terrorist suspects" by November 2001, but few were convicted of any actual crimes.[9]

Meanwhile, some state police apparently became confused about their mission, as others had during the civil rights and Vietnam War eras. In the guise of pursuing terrorists, Maryland State Police mounted surveillance

THE NEWHALL MASSACRE

The California Highway Patrol (CHP) ranks as one of America's 10 most danger-prone law enforcement agencies, with 216 officers killed between 1923 and 2008. Of those deaths, 148 were accidental, most involving vehicular crashes, but 68 officers were murdered in the line of duty.[10] The CHP's worst single day was April 6, 1970, remembered in California as the date of the "Newhall massacre."

The incident began when Bobby Davis, a 27-year-old career criminal, made an illegal U-turn in the middle of U.S. Highway 99, nearly striking a car occupied by Jack and Pamela Tidwell. The Tidwells confronted Davis, who threatened them with a pistol, then fled the scene. Jack Tidwell telephoned the CHP, and a search began. By the time Officers Walt Frago and Roger Gore spotted Davis's car on the highway, Davis had picked up Jack Twinning, his 35-year-old partner in crime. Davis stopped his car on command, and then he and Twinning opened fire, killing both officers instantly.

Seconds after Frago and Gore were gunned down, CHP Officers George Alleyn and James Pence arrived on the scene. A second shootout began, with Officers Alleyn and Pence slain on the spot, while Twinning sustained a minor wound on nonviolent activists who protested capital punishment, global warming, nuclear testing, and the U.S. invasion of Iraq. Superintendent Terrence Sheridan admitted that his department had submitted names of 53 innocent persons, including two elderly Catholic nuns, for inclusion in FBI terrorist files. "The names don't belong in there," Sheridan told U.S. Senate investigators in October 2008. "It's as simple as that." *Time* magazine reporter Robert Baer covered that hearing and wrote, "You have to wonder how many more lists like Maryland's are out there." His question was answered—at least in part—from Michigan, where state police had reported other nonviolent groups to FBI headquarters, including the East Lansing Animal Rights Movement, the Coalition to Defend Affirmative Action, and Direct Action, a nonviolent antiwar group.[11]

to his forehead. A passing driver, 31-year-old Gary Kness, stopped to help the patrolmen and wounded Davis with a shot from Officer Pence's revolver before the gunmen fled on foot, each running in a different direction.

At 3:25 A.M. on April 7, Davis stumbled onto a camper occupied by Daniel Schwartz, who traded shots with Davis before the gunman overpowered him and fled in Schwartz's truck. Schwartz telephoned authorities, and Davis surrendered to Los Angeles County sheriff's deputies several hours later. Meanwhile, Twinning invaded the home of Stephen Hoag, three miles from the Newhall murder scene, holding Hoag, his wife and son hostage at gunpoint. Hoag's wife had time to call police before she was captured, and officers soon surrounded the house. Twinning released his prisoners at 9:00 A.M., but refused to surrender. He shot himself as police fired tear gas into the house.

Bobby Davis was sentenced to die for the murders, but his sentence was commuted to life imprisonment without parole in 1972, when the U.S. Supreme Court invalidated all standing death sentences nationwide, in the case of *Furman v. Georgia*. Analysis of the shootout prompted changes in CHP firearms policy. Patrolmen retained their six-shot revolvers, but received speed loaders to aid with reloading in emergencies.

5

The Feds

Barrington, Illinois

Bank robber "Baby Face" Nelson had trouble with names. Born Lester Gillis in 1908, he found the name unmanly and began to call himself George Nelson—preferring "Big George," though he stood only 5 feet, 4¾ inches tall. His youthful features worked against him, and after a witness to one of his holdups described him as "baby-faced," reporters tagged him with the nickname he despised.

Still, there was nothing childish about Nelson's violent temper. He was an expert gunman, blamed for several murders. He killed FBI agent Carter Baum and wounded two other lawmen in April 1934, during a shootout in Wisconsin. By November, following the violent deaths of outlaws John Dillinger and Charles "Pretty Boy" Floyd, Nelson was ranked as America's "Public Enemy No. 1."

On November 17, 1934, FBI Agents Samuel Cowley and Herman Hollis spotted Nelson driving through Barrington, a Chicago suburb, with his wife and sidekick John Paul Chase. They pursued him, trading gunfire, until Nelson's damaged car swerved off the highway and a pitched battle ensued. Firing a machine gun, Nelson killed both agents, but not before they wounded him repeatedly. After escaping in their car, Nelson collapsed and died. His corpse was found next morning, dumped outside a local cemetery. Two thousand people came to view his body at Chicago's morgue.

IN THE BEGINNING

While the U.S. Constitution established itself as the "supreme Law of the land" in 1788, it provided no mechanism for its own enforcement.[1] The Judiciary Act of 1789 created the Attorney General's office, assigned "to prosecute and conduct all suits in the Supreme Court in which the United States shall be concerned"—but again, no agency existed to assist him. The U.S. Department of Justice would not be created until 1870.

President George Washington (1732–99) recognized the problem, telling first Attorney General Edmund Randolph that "the due administration of justice is the firmest pillar of good Government." With that in mind, Washington ordered recruitment of "the fittest characters to expound the law and dispense justice" in the original 13 states.[2] Thus, the U.S. Marshals Service was created as America's first federal law enforcement agency, chosing its early members from the ranks of Revolutionary War veterans.

Those early marshals shared numerous duties. Aside from investigating federal crimes and pursuing fugitives, they supervised incarceration, transportation, and execution of federal prisoners; served writs, subpoenas, summonses, and warrants issued by federal courts; disbursed funds as ordered by federal judges; managed the budget and payroll for federal courts; hired court bailiffs, criers, and janitors; rented space for federal courtrooms and jails; and supervised the conduct of federal trials. Outside of the nation's capital, U.S. Marshals represented the federal government in towns from coast to coast, as the country expanded westward. They published presidential proclamations, collected commercial statistics, and took the U.S. census from 1790 to 1870, when responsibility for that duty shifted to the Executive Branch of government.

As if those tasks did not consume enough time and energy, Congress constantly added new chores to the list. Until 1865, when the Secret Service was created, U.S. Marshals pursued counterfeiters who passed "funny money." They joined in suppressing the 1794 Whiskey Rebellion and enforced federal liquor laws until the 1920s, when the Treasury Department took over. Between 1850 and 1861, marshals enforced the unpopular Fugitive Slave Act, facing violence from abolitionists when they returned runaways to their owners. In the Wild West, U.S. Marshals pursued America's most notorious bandits, including the Dalton brothers, Bill Doolin, Ned Christie, and Billy the Kid. Marshal Henry White spent four years in West Virginia, trying to resolve a bloody feud between the Hatfields and McCoys. During the Civil War and World War I, marshals tracked foreign spies and saboteurs, draft dodgers, and "enemy aliens."

Modern U.S. Marshals handle an equally wide range of duties. Between 1957 and 1965, when the FBI refused to protect civil rights activists or black students in newly integrated schools, marshals filled the gap. Most such assignments passed without bloodshed, but 166 marshals were injured—including 30 wounded by gunfire—during a riot at the University of Mississippi, in September 1962.[3] Five years later, 300 marshals confronted 35,000 antiwar demonstrators at the Pentagon, arresting 682 persons.[4] The Special Operations Group, America's oldest SWAT team, was created in 1971 to deal with incidents on government property, including riots at federal prisons and the 1973 occupation of Wounded Knee, South Dakota, by members of the American Indian Movement. In 1971 Congress established the Witness Security Program, assigning U.S. Marshals to protect federal witnesses in hiding. Since its inception, the program has absorbed more than 7,500 witnesses and 9,500 of their relatives.[5]

Pursuit of federal fugitives remains a major task of the U.S. Marshals Service, which created its first Fugitive Instestigation Strike Team in 1981. Between 2005 and 2007, Operation Falcon captured 59,177 fugitive felons.[6] Many of those arrests came through sting operations, trapping fugitives with appeals to their greed in the form of "prizes" from fictitious contests.

THE NOT-SO-SECRET SERVICE

The "secret service" label normally applies to spies or police conducting covert—and sometimes illegal—operations against rival nations. The U.S. Secret Service is unique in that regard, as a law enforcement agency that pursues much of its business in the spotlight of publicity.

Congress created the Secret Service in July 1865, as a branch of the U.S. Treasury Department. Chief William Wood and his agents were assigned to suppress counterfeit currency, which had proliferated during the Civil War. Two years later, Secret Service duties expanded to include "detecting persons perpetrating frauds against the government"—a broad directive that launched investigations of the terrorist Ku Klux Klan, moonshiners, smugglers, mail robbers, and other federal offenders.

Today, Secret Service agents are best known for protecting U.S. presidents, other federal officials or candidates for office, and visiting foreign leaders, but the early service performed no such tasks. Agents first assumed informal, part-time responsibility for presidential security in 1894, during the second term of President Grover Cleveland. None were present when anarchist Leon Czolgosz shot President William McKinley in September 1901, but the assassination prompted a congressional request for full-time protection, beginning in 1902. Congress authorized protection of the president-elect in 1913, and President Warren Harding created a new Secret Service unit, the White House Police Force, in 1922. In the 1960s protection duties expanded to cover ex-presidents and their families, presidential candidates, vice presidents, and vice presidents-elect. Still, no system is perfect, as witnessed by the assassination of President John F. Kennedy in 1963 and the wounding of President Ronald Reagan in 1981.

While executive protection has eclipsed all other Secret Service duties in the public mind, the agency continues its pursuit of counterfeiters worldwide. In 1984 Congress authorized the Secret Service to investigate violations of federal laws concerning identity theft, credit or debit card fraud, and computer fraud. Between 2003 and 2008, agents arrested nearly 29,000 persons for counterfeiting, computer violations, and other financial crimes, securing a 98 percent conviction rate. In the process, they seized more than $295 million in counterfeit currency and prevented financial losses exceeding $12 billion.[7]

"G-MEN"

In 1908 Attorney General Charles Bonaparte sought to create a new detective force within the Justice Department. Congressional leaders refused to approve it, voicing fears of an illegal domestic spy network, but Bonaparte waited until Congress took its next recess, and then created the team anyway. President Theodore Roosevelt supported the move, and congressional fears were soon realized, as the fledgling agency harassed various labor leaders, "radicals," and "militant" racial minorities.

Bonaparte's unit was nameless for a year, then became the Bureau of Investigation (1909–1932), the U.S. Bureau of Investigation (1932–33), the Division of Investigation (1933–35), and finally the Federal Bureau of Investigation. Its original duties involved investigation of land fraud, antitrust violations, bankruptcy frauds, and peonage (slavery). Between 1910 and 1934 that list expanded to include "white slavery," kidnapping, bank robbery, interstate transportation of stolen property, and interstate flight to avoid prosecution or prison. At the same time, FBI agents continued unauthorized surveillance of "subversives" nationwide, ranging from average citizens to congressmen and federal judges.

Despite its far-flung net, few Americans knew anything about the FBI before July 17, 1933, when one agent died and two others suffered wounds in a chaotic gunfight dubbed the "Kansas City Massacre." Over the next three years agents pursued a short list of bandits and kidnappers known in the press as "public enemies." That federal "crime war" claimed nine lives—six fugitives and three agents[8]—while making the bureau world famous. It also gave agents a new nickname—"G-men," for *government men*—coined by an FBI publicist and falsely credited to outlaw George "Machine Gun" Kelly.

The FBI claims that its brief crime war "resulted in the arrest or demise of all the major gangsters by 1936,"[9] but in fact, the bureau ignored the real major gangsters of organized crime until the early 1960s, insisting that no national syndicate existed. By 1936 the FBI had shifted most of its attention back to politics, shadowing communists and fascists under orders from President Franklin Roosevelt. Director J. Edgar Hoover seized the opportunity to spy on anyone whose private life or views on government offended him. By the end of World War II, Hoover's secret files held so much "dirt" on prominent Americans, including presidents, that few were brave enough to criticize him publicly before his death in 1972.

The "new" FBI made dramatic changes, including recruitment of the first "G-women" hired since Hoover forced Agent Lenore Houston's resignation in 1928. Minority hiring also increased, while the bureau

J. Edgar Hoover, the best-known director of the Federal Bureau of Investigation, poses in his office in Washington in 1965. *AP Photo*

revised its targets and tactics. Mobsters faced RICO Act charges, while corrupt politicians and union leaders were snared in undercover "sting" operations. Agent Joseph Pistone, alias "Donnie Brasco," infiltrated New York City's Bonnano and Colombo Mafia families, producing more than 100 convictions. Cyberthieves and serial killers also received attention after the collapse of Russian communism in 1991 ended the four-decade Cold War.

The terrorist attacks of September 2001 changed everything. Overnight, the FBI shifted its priorities from "normal" crimes to prevention of terrorism. While it claims success, citing the lack of any serious attacks on U.S. soil since 9/11, critics note that by 2007 the number of criminal cases filed by FBI agents had dropped 34 percent, white-collar arrests declined by 90 percent, while investigation of hate crimes and

J. EDGAR HOOVER (1895–1972)

John Edgar Hoover was born in Washington, D.C., reportedly on January 1, 1895. (Questions linger because his birth certificate was not officially filed until 1938.) After earning a law degree in 1917, Hoover worked at the Library of Congress and then switched to the Justice Department. During World War I he led the department's Enemy Aliens Registration Section, and in 1919 he headed the General Intelligence Division, coordinating a nationwide series of "Red raids" that deported hundreds of suspected communists and anarchists.

In 1921 Hoover joined the Bureau of Investigation (later the FBI) as its deputy chief. Scandals were rife during the corrupt administration of President Warren Harding, which saw the Justice Department nicknamed "the Department of Easy Virtue," and while Hoover was involved in some of the illegal activity, he preserved a public façade of scrupulous ethics. In 1924 he was named to lead the bureau, and he maintained that post until his death, 48 years later.

Hoover is famous for cleaning up the scandalized FBI and making it one of the world's most professional law enforcement agencies. He fired many corrupt political appointees, created the famous FBI Laboratory and the FBI Academy (which also trains police officers from various states and foreign nations), while promoting agents with college degrees in law or accounting. During his half-century as FBI director, Hoover's agents crushed bank-robbing gangs in the 1930s, arrested Nazi saboteurs during World War II, pursued Russian spies during the Cold War, and jailed members of the terrorist Ku Klux Klan in Southern states. For decades Hoover stood as America's "top cop," an icon hailed by law-and-order patriots from coast to coast.

police misconduct dropped 65 percent.[10] Despite increased surveillance on suspected terrorists, those critics say the bureau has gone overboard, granting virtual immunity to countless felons.

Sadly, there was a darker side to Hoover and his FBI. Today it is known that Hoover obstructed civil rights enforcement and harassed minority activists. In extreme cases, documented by FBI files, some agents even supplied weapons to rival "radical" groups, in hopes that the members would kill each other. (Some did.) Other targets of Hoover's included liberal reporters and writers, actors and musicians, political figures and labor leaders. Between 1960 and 1972, FBI agents admittedly carried out 1,992 illegal wiretaps, planted 605 unauthorized listening devices, and stole at least 54,574 pieces of personal mail.[11]

At the same time, Hoover ignored an ever-expanding national crime syndicate. In the early 1950s, while the IRS and Federal Bureau of Narcotics pursued gangsters nationwide, he assigned agents "to determine and document the nonexistence of organized crime."[12] Some researchers claim he was afraid mobsters would corrupt the FBI, as they did other agencies, but other reports have revealed Hoover's private friendship with various wealthy gangsters. Criminals favored him with tips on fixed horse races, bankrolled his investments in various companies, and donated large amounts of money to Hoover's favorite charities—including the J. Edgar Hoover Foundation, established in 1965.

While Hoover faced increasing criticism in his final years, most of his abuses were not fully revealed until after his death, at age 77, in May 1972. Despite protests from certain congressmen whom Hoover had blackmailed, the FBI's present headquarters, completed in 1974, bears his name. With Hoover in mind, federal law now forbids any individual from serving more than 10 years as the FBI's director.

CONTROLLING SUBSTANCES

Whether its interest is simple tax collection or a judgment on "morality," the federal government has always meddled in the production, sale and possession of intoxicating substances. A federal tax on whiskey, imposed in 1791, sparked the republic's first armed rebellion three years later. Regulation of other intoxicants followed from 1914 onward, requiring creation of more agencies to detect and punish the newly banned acts.

For decades Congress used its taxing power as a weapon against "evil" drugs.

The Harrison Narcotics Tax Act of 1914 regulated opiates and cocaine by forcing producers and dealers to register with Washington and pay tax on their earnings. The Marihuana Tax Act of 1937 extended those rules to cannabis. Emphasis on taxation delegated enforcement to the U.S. Treasury Department, pursued by agents of the Internal Revenue Service (IRS).

The advent of Prohibition required creation of a special unit to keep America "dry." Despite its vast domain, the bureau started small, beginning with 1,520 agents in 1920 and growing to 2,836 by 1930. Unfortunately, most failed to meet the standard of the bureau's most famous agent, Chicago's "untouchable" Eliot Ness. By 1930, the bureau had hired 17,816 agents and fired 13,513 for taking bribes. The end result was predictable: Americans drank freely at 500,000 illegal saloons, while millionaire bootleggers organized criminal networks spanning the nation.[13]

While Prohibition floundered, Secretary of the Treasury Andrew Mellon tried to do better with drugs. He created a Narcotic Division in 1921 and a Federal Narcotics Board in 1922, and then merged them in 1930 as the Federal Bureau of Narcotics (FBN). Director Harry Anslinger (1892–1975) led the FBN from its inception until 1962, pursuing drug dealers and addicts with a zeal some critics called obsession. Unlike J. Edgar Hoover, Anslinger recognized and publicized the role of organized crime in drug trafficking, earning Hoover's lifelong hatred in the process. His lobbying in Congress secured passage of new laws, including the Opium Poppy Control Act of 1942, the 1951 Boggs Act (imposing mandatory sentences for drug offenses), and the 1956 Narcotics Control Act (increasing the Boggs Act sentences). While

ELMER IREY (1888–1948)

Elmer Irey was the polar opposite of J. Edgar Hoover, a lawman who shunned publicity while leading the IRS Enforcement Branch from 1919 to 1941. Despite that modesty—or because of it—Irey and his "T-men" (for *Treasury men*) proved remarkably effective in jailing the organized mobsters whom Hoover's FBI persistently ignored. During Prohibition, when corruption and terror prevented conviction of major bootleggers for liquor violations, Irey attacked them with charges of income tax evasion and sent some of the syndicate's top men to prison. Those convicted included Chicago's "Scarface" Al Capone and various subordinates, Cleveland's Morris Kleinman, New Jersey's Irving "Waxey Gordon" Wexler, and millionaire bookmaker Moses Annenberg. Over the course of his career, Irey obtained indictments on more than 15,000 tax-dodgers, scoring a 90-percent conviction rate.[14]

Irey also played a central role in America's most famous kidnapping case. When young Charles Lindbergh Jr. was snatched in 1932, Irey suggested paying the ransom in obsolete gold certificates. That ploy eventually led to the arrest of suspect Bruno Hauptmann, caught with $14,590 of the ransom money in 1934. Hauptmann was later convicted of murder and executed in 1936. Today, some researchers question his guilt, but possession of the ransom money sealed his fate. Ironically, FBI spokesmen later claimed credit for solving the Lindbergh case, although the bureau did not take charge of the investigation until October 1933, while Hauptmann was arrested by officers of the New York Police Department and New Jersey State Police, without FBI participation.

supporters of drug prohibition hailed those achievements, critics noted that Anslinger's focus on marijuana, including collaboration on Hollywood films such as *Damaged Lives* (1930) and *Reefer Madness* (1936), created a national hysteria divorced from scientific reality.

With Prohibition's repeal, the Treasury Department created a new Alcohol Tax Unit to pursue unlicensed liquor manufacturers, renamed the Alcohol and Tobacco Tax Division when its duties expanded in 1951, then reborn in 1972 as the Bureau of Alcohol, Tobacco and Firearms. (Assorted "gangster weapons"—machine guns, sawed-off shotguns and silencers—had been subject to federal tax and registration since 1934.) Following 9/11, the ATF was moved from the Treasury to the Justice Department, with its title changed to the Bureau of Alcohol, Tobacco, Firearms and Explosives. The late addition emphasized the ATF's investigation of domestic bombings, which in fact began with passage of the 1970 Explosives Control Act. In January 2003 the task of collecting federal alcohol and tobacco taxes shifted to the Treasury Department's new Alcohol and Tobacco Tax and Trade Bureau. The ATF retained jurisdiction over smuggling of untaxed liquor and tobacco, while placing greater emphasis on weapons and explosives violations.

Another agency created by President Richard Nixon in 1972, the Office of Drug Abuse Law Enforcement (ODALE), was established to coordinate state and federal antidrug efforts. Dissatisfied with its progress 12 months later, Nixon merged the ODALE with the older Bureau of Narcotics and Dangerous Drugs to create a new Drug Enforcement Administration (DEA) under Director John Bartels. The DEA was launched with 1,470 agents and a budget of $65.2 million, but it grew swiftly. By 1974 it had 43 foreign offices in 31 countries and a budget of $116 million. Today, the DEA employs 5,235 agents and 5,500 civilian employees, with 87 foreign offices in 61 nations, and enjoys a budget of $2.4 billion.[15] In 2007 DEA agents arrested 27,780 persons, raided 5,910 illegal methamphetamine labs, and seized vast quantities of illicit drugs, including 784,238 pounds of marijuana, 212,769 pounds of cocaine, 2,389 pounds of methamphetamine, 1,375 pounds of heroin, and 5,636,305 doses of hallucinogenic substances.[16]

GUARDING BORDERS

Over the past 220 years various federal agencies have shouldered the burden of securing America's borders against smugglers and unwelcome aliens. First was the U.S. Customs Service, created in July 1789 to collect taxes on imported goods. Until 1913, when the Constitution's Sixteenth Amendment created a federal income tax, customs duties provided most of the government's income. In later years Customs agents also played a leading role in intercepting various forms of contraband, ranging from outlawed liquor (during Prohibition) and drugs to child pornography.

In June 1870 Congress created the U.S. Immigration and Naturalization Service (INS) as a branch of the Justice Department, assigned to supervise legal immigration and deport aliens who entered the country illegally. Various federal statutes—including the Chinese Exclusion Act of 1882, the Emergency Quota Act of 1921, the Immigration Act of 1924, and the McCarran-Walter Act of 1952—established preferences and quotas for immigrants from various countries, which the INS was bound to enforce. In 1954, for example, the INS launched Operation Wetback, intended to purge millions of illegal Mexican immigrants from the Southwest. While highly publicized, such efforts rarely succeeded, in large part because wealthy farmers and other employers demanded cheap immigrant labor. The U.S. Border Patrol, created in 1924, served as the primary INS enforcement arm, with most of its agents assigned to surveillance along the Mexican border. A unique subdivision of the Border Patrol, dubbed the "Shadow Wolves," consists of Native American trackers employed since 1972 to hunt smugglers crossing the border from Mexico into Arizona's Tohono O'odham Indian Reservation.

As with other federal agencies, America's border guardians found their lives radically changed by the 9/11 terrorist attacks. The old INS was disbanded, its former naturalization duties shifting to a new U.S. Citizenship and Immigration Service, while its enforcement arm merged with Customs to become U.S. Immigration and Customs Enforcement (ICE). The Border Patrol's agents were likewise divided, with some assigned to the ICE, while others found themselves serving with U.S. Customs and Border Protection. If the new plan seemed confusing and redundant, at least the several units answered to a single master, combined as they were within the Department of Homeland Security. Other agencies beneath that broad umbrella include the Secret Service, the U.S. Coast Guard, the Transportation Security Administration, the Federal Emergency Management Agency, the Animal and Plant Health Inspection Service, and the U.S. Federal Protective Service (assigned to guard 9,000 government buildings nationwide).

LOOSE ENDS

The groups described above by no means exhaust the list of 87 active federal law enforcement agencies.[17] Some others include:

- The Federal Air Marshal Service, created in 1968 as the Federal Aviation Administration's Sky Marshal Program, to end a rash of airline hijackings by criminals seeking free passage to foreign countries. Air marshals are trained at the FBI Academy in Quantico, Virginia, and armed with weapons designed to kill or disable humans, without causing aircraft to suffer sudden decompression and crash as a result. Today, Air Marshals serve the Transportation Security Administration, as part of the Homeland Security Department.

- The Tennessee Valley Authority Police patrol property owned by the TVA, established in 1933 and presently responsible for 29 hydroelectric dams, 11 fossil-fuel plants, six combustion turbine plants, and three nuclear power plants spanning seven states. TVA recreation facilities also serve 100 million visitors per year.[18]

- The U.S. Federal Reserve Police, assigned to protect America's central banking network. Established in 1913, the Federal Reserve System consists of 12 regional banks located in Boston, New York City, Philadelphia, Dallas, Cleveland, Chicago, Minneapolis, St. Louis, Atlanta, San Francisco, Kansas City (Missouri), and Richmond, Virginia.

Crime Beyond Borders

6

Mexico City

The news was stunning. On December 3, 2008, the newspaper *El Universal* reported that Mexico had recorded 5,031 murders linked to organized crime since January 1—an average of 15 slayings per day, without counting murders prompted by other motives or the many crimes that Mexican police admit go unreported every year. The gang-related death toll represented a 70-percent increase from 2005, when authorities blamed organized crime for 1,500 murders nationwide.[1]

In fact, crime had become so bad in Mexico that vigilante groups were striking back. In Guerrero, where authorities held a man suspected of killing three policemen, a lynch mob dragged him from jail, beheaded him, and left his head beside a major highway. On December 1 police found nine decapitated bodies in Tijuana, just across the border from San Diego, California. Meanwhile, in Ciudad Juarez—across the Rio Grande from El Paso, Texas—more than 400 women have been kidnapped, raped and murdered since 1993, with others still missing and most of the slayings unsolved.[2]

Part of Mexico's problem is the vast illegal drug trade, which has corrupted law enforcement nationwide and turned some police into underworld contract killers. Mexico's Federal Judicial Police department was so riddled with corruption that President Vicente Fox abolished it in 2003, creating a new Federal Investigative Agency (AFI) supervised by the Attorney General's office. Still, the problem continued. In 2004

69

AFI regional director Armando Villalobos and 26 other officers were arrested in Cancun. In April 2008 authorities in Nuevo Leon charged 141 state officers with participation in drug smuggling by the notorious Gulf Cartel. Two months later, Public Safety Secretary Genaro Garcia Luna announced mandatory drug and polygraph (lie detector) tests for 284 AFI officers, with dismissal awaiting any who failed.[3]

A WORLD OF CRIME

While criminals have never paid much attention to borders, except where crossing a line on a map prevents their arrest, the world's 193 recognized sovereign nations define themselves by political boundaries.[4] Violation of those borders by a foreign power is an act of war, while intrusion of foreign spies constitutes the serious crime of espionage. Pursuing criminals who operate between countries—whether the case involves a lone fugitive or a gang with thousands of members—demands cooperation between different governments and law enforcement agencies.

International law is a broad term referring to various agreements made between nations for mutual benefit and protection. Common features of international law include mutual respect for borders during peacetime, decent care for prisoners of war, protection of embassies and diplomats, prosecution of pirates, and respect for various treaties which may include extradition (legal surrender) of international fugitives.

Enforcement of international law is often difficult, even where binding treaties are in force, since no universally recognized global police force or judicial system exists. The pressure to conform and to abide by certain rules of conduct comes primarily from diplomats and "world opinion," which any sovereign state is free to ignore. Where negotiations fail, large nations may impose sanctions (penalties, such as cutting off aid or supplies) on smaller states, or may invade by force, at the risk of provoking armed response from opponents.

Since World War I various countries have attempted to enforce treaties and keep world peace through international alliances. The first such group in modern times, the League of Nations (1919–46), tried to resolve territorial disputes, suppress drug trafficking, and eliminate slavery, but it possessed no mechanism for enforcement and effectively collapsed with the outbreak of World War II in 1939. The League's Permanent Court of International Justice heard 38 cases and issued 27 advisory opinions between 1922 and 1940, but none related to criminal matters.[5]

The first international criminal trials occurred after World War II, when the victorious Allies prosecuted German and Japanese prisoners accused of war crimes. In Germany a series of 502 trials examined 1,700 defendants. Of those, 309 were condemned (with 294 executed) and 1,702 received various prison terms. In Japan trials held for 5,728 defendants ended with 991 condemned and 3,437 imprisoned.[6]

The United Nations (UN), formed in 1946, replaced the League of Nations with an organization wielding greater authority. Its Security Council maintains a force military of peacekeepers—often called "Blue Helmets" for their distinctive headgear—who strive to prevent violence in war-torn nations, but the team is widely criticized for its failures, including its inability to prevent or halt the 1994 Rwandan genocide, the 1995 Srebenica massacre in Bosnia and Herzegovina, the Second Congo War of 1998-2003, the genocidal conflict occurring in Darfur, Sudan, since 2003, and the ongoing Somalian civil war that began in 2006. While various UN resolutions and conventions (international agreements) condemn slavery and global traffic in drugs or weapons, the UN has no police force of its own.

INTERPOL

The first step toward coordinated global law enforcement came in 1923, with creation of the International Criminal Police. Based in Austria, the group streamlined communications between police of various member nations, but its effectiveness was compromised when Adolf Hitler's Nazis seized control of Austria in 1938. Agents of Hitler's Gestapo (Secret State Police) took command of the ICP, using it to track fugitive Jews and other "enemies" of Germany, while generally ignoring common criminals. British and Canadian police abandoned the ICP when World War II began, and the FBI withdrew in 1941, a year before Hitler transferred ICP headquarters to Berlin.

In 1945 victorious European Allies—including Britain, Belgium, France, and the nations of Scandinavia—revived the organization

Nigerian peacekeepers with the United Nations and African Union mission to stop the genocide in Darfur prepare for a patrol. The peacekeepers are easily recognized by their distinctive blue helmets. *AP Photo/Alfred de Montesquiou*

with a new name: the International Criminal Police Organization, better known as Interpol. Its headquarters stood in Saint-Cloud, a suburb of Paris, until 1989, when the main office moved 244 miles east, to Lyon.

As of 2008, 187 nations belong to Interpol, coordinating information and activities in the "priority crime areas of fugitives, public safety and terrorism, drugs and organized crime, trafficking in human beings, and financial and high-tech crime." Interpol maintains a global police communications system called I-24/7, which provides police of member nations with a forum for exchanging data on crime and criminals. As described in its mission statement, Interpol further "provides focused police training initiatives for national police forces, and also offers on-demand advice, guidance, and support in building dedicated crime-fighting components. The aim is to enhance the capacity of member countries to effectively combat serious transnational crime and terrorism." With the Nazi era in mind, Interpol's constitution strictly forbids "any intervention or activities of a political, military, religious or racial character."[7]

Advisory and training functions aside, Interpol's officers also conduct investigations and arrest criminals. Some of its well-known cases include:

- The August 2004 arrest of Suzan Tamim, a Lebanese singer accused of fleeing to Egypt with $350,000 stolen from her husband, Adel Matouq.
- The October 2007 arrest in Bangkok, Thailand, of Canadian schoolteacher Christopher Paul Neil, indicted for sexual abuse of young Asian boys.
- Operation SOGA (for *Soccer Gambling*), a six-month sting operation that climaxed with raids on 262 illegal gambling dens in China, Malaysia, Singapore, Thailand, and Vietnam. In all, 423 persons were arrested, while Interpol agents and local police seized $680,000 in cash, plus computers, mobile telephones, bank cards, and vehicles.[8]
- The May 2008 arrest of Wayne Nelson Corliss in Union City, New Jersey, on charges of sexually abusing young boys in Thailand. Agents identified Corliss—an actor who earned some of his income by performing at children's parties—from pornographic photos posted on the Internet.

Despite such successes, Interpol still suffers occasional embarrassment. In 1989 the agency's top officer in Mexico, Florentino Ventura Gutierrez, was exposed as a member of a drug-dealing cult that practiced human sacrifice. Nineteen years later, in November 2008, Mexican police arrested Ricardo Gutiérrez Vargas—Mexico's Interpol liaison officer and the AFI's Director for International Police Affairs—for selling classified information to members of notorious drug cartels.

INTERPOL'S COMPETITION

At the time of this writing, two other international police agencies competed with Interpol for a role in global law enforcement. The older of the two is Europol—the European Police Office—which serves as a criminal intelligence agency for the European Union (EU). Consisting of 27 member nations, the EU was created by the Maastricht Treaty in February 1992 and became an effective unit on November 1, 1993. Europol began limited operations in January 1994, as the Europol

Immigration and Customs Enforcement agents escort pedophile Wayne Nelson Corliss from his apartment building in Union, New Jersey, after his arrest on May 8. Corliss was arrested two days after Interpol made an appeal for public help in the international manhunt to catch him. *AP Photo/via Immigration and Customs Enforcement*

Drugs Unit, but the Europol Convention was not formally ratified until June 1998. The agency officially "opened" on October 1, 1998, but was not deemed fully operational until July 1, 1999.[9]

Europol's stated mission is to "make a significant contribution to the European Union's law enforcement action in preventing and combating terrorism, unlawful drug trafficking and other serious forms of international crime within its competencies, with a particular emphasis on the criminal organizations involved." In October 1998 the group deemed itself "competent to prevent and combat unlawful drug trafficking, trafficking in nuclear and radioactive substances, illegal immigrant smuggling, trade in human beings, motor vehicle crime and associated money laundering activities." Europol's mandate was later extended to include terrorism and other forms of serious international crime.[10]

Based at The Hague in the Netherlands, Europol maintains a staff of 612, including 118 liaison officers, supported by a budget of 66.4 million euros in 2008. A Council of Ministers for Justice and Home Affairs supervises the group's operations. Despite its broad mission statement, Europol wields no direct police powers itself. Rather, it was conceived and operates today as a clearinghouse for information, facilitating communication between EU member states and a list of other nations, including Albania, Australia, Bosnia and Herzegovina, Canada, Colombia, Croatia, Iceland, Macedonia, Moldova, Norway, the Russian Federation, Switzerland, Turkey, and the United States.[11]

Europol's counterpart in the Western Hemisphere is the American Police Community, also called Ameripol. Representatives from 18 nations met in Bogotá, Colombia, to create Ameripol on November 14, 2007. General Óscar Adolfo Naranjo, commander of the Colombian National Police, was named to lead Ameripol until 2010, when election of successors to three-year terms shall begin. Current member states include Argentina, Bolivia, Brazil, Chile, Colombia, Costa Rica, Cuba, the Dominican Republic, Ecuador, El Salvador, Guatemala, Haiti, Honduras, Jamaica, Mexico, Paraguay, Peru, and Uruguay.

Like Europol, Ameripol has no direct police authority. Instead, it coordinates exchange of information on matters including drug and arms trafficking, illegal immigration or human trafficking, terrorism, war crimes, money laundering, corporate crime, copyright infringement, computer crime, and child pornography. While the United States is not a member, many of Ameripol's members cooperate with the DEA and FBI. All of Ameripol's 18 member states are also Interpol members.

EXTRADITION VS. RENDITION

Retrieving fugitives from foreign countries has been a problem throughout history. Outlaws from America's Old West often fled to Mexico, while draft evaders found refuge in Canada during the Vietnam War. Rival nations frequently refuse extradition out of spite, and some accuse their neighbors of actively supporting smuggling and terrorism. Nations that have abandoned capital punishment, such as Britain and Canada, commonly refuse extradition of fugitives facing execution elsewhere. Most countries offer *asylum* (protection) to refugees from nations they deem cruel, corrupt, or tyrannical.

Since 1901 the U.S. government has signed formal extradition treaties with 110 foreign countries.[12] Some of those nations, like Yugoslavia, no longer exist. In others, such as Cuba, changes in political leadership and philosophy canceled the treaties. A majority of African and Asian countries have no extradition treaties with America, and even certain "friendly" states, such as Saudi Arabia, balk at putting any formal agreement on paper.

Where no extradition treaties exist, and foreign leaders refuse to negotiate extradition, nations seeking to arrest fugitives sometimes resort to illegal methods. Israel pioneered such techniques in 1960 when its agents kidnapped Nazi war criminal Adolf Eichmann from Argentina and smuggled him halfway around the world for trial and execution in Jerusalem. In 1972, following the terrorist slaughter of Israeli athletes at the Munich Olympic Games, Tel Aviv launched Operation Wrath of God to assassinate persons deemed responsible for the attack. Such killings—regarded as "self-defense" by Israelis, condemned as murder in the nations where they occur—continue to the present day, with the execution of several targets acknowledged in June 2008.[13]

While the U.S. Central Intelligence Agency (CIA) practiced or attempted assassination of various foreign leaders in the 1960s, ordinary criminals who fled the country were exempt until President Ronald

Reagan took office. In 1984 and 1986, despite a total lack of legal jurisdiction, Congress passed laws imposing federal penalties on terrorists
who hijack airplanes or attack American citizens in foreign countries.
In 1985, after gunmen seized the Italian cruise ship *Achille Lauro* and
killed an American passenger, U.S. Navy jets forced their getaway plane
to land at an airbase in Sicily, but Italian troops prevented removal
of the perpetrators. A year later President Reagan secretly authorized
kidnapping of indicted terrorists wherever they were found. The first
known incident occurred in 1987, after the hijacking of a Jordanian
airliner with American passengers aboard. FBI agents lured ringleader
Fawaz Yunis into international waters on the Mediterranean Sea, then
arrested him and flew him back to the United States, where he received
a 30-year prison term. Such kidnappings were soon labeled rendition.

President Bill Clinton continued Reagan's rendition policy with a
directive signed in 1995. According to Richard Clarke, Clinton's chief
counterterrorism advisor to the U.S. National Security Council, Clinton debated the legality of rendition with Vice President Al Gore and
congressional leaders, deciding to proceed after Gore declared, "That's
a no-brainer. Of course it's a violation of international law, that's why it's
a covert action. The guy is a terrorist. Go grab his ass."[14]

According to CIA veteran Michael Scheuer's testimony before
Congress in April 2007, covert kidnapping entered a new phase called
extraordinary rendition in 1995. Under that program, suspected terrorists were snatched in foreign countries and flown to Egypt for interrogation, where U.S. legal bans on torture do not apply. Federal law requires
our government to seek "assurances" that rendered suspects will not be
tortured, but Scheuer denied that any formal agreements to that effect
were signed, while admitting that Egyptian treatment of prisoners is
"not up to U.S. standards."[15]

Extraordinary rendition reached its controversial height—or
depth—after the 9/11 terrorist attacks, when President George W. Bush
declared a global War on Terror. No statistics are available, and Bush
administration spokesmen wavered for years over definitions of "torture," but reporter Dana Priest described a typical rendition operation
in the *Washington Post*.

"MERCHANT OF DEATH"

Mystery surrounds the life of Victor Anatolyevich Bout, beginning with his birth in 1967. Conflicting reports claim that he was born either in Turkmenistan or in the Tajik Soviet Socialist Republic (now Tajikistan). He definitely served as a major in the Soviet GRU (military intelligence) and then retired in 1993 to become one of the world's richest and most notorious arms dealers, known as the "Embargo Buster" and the "Merchant of Death."

Bout's first nickname derived from smuggling weapons into African nations facing an embargo (ban) on sale of military hardware imposed by the United Nations. Those embargoes were established in an effort to stop long-running civil wars and prevent genocide, but profit came first for the Merchant of Death. Fluent in six languages, he founded the Transavia Export Cargo Company, buying surplus Russian weapons and selling them to the highest bidders. By 1995 Bout had made $50 million selling arms to rival groups in Afghanistan alone. He then formed the Trans Aviation Network Group, based in Belgium, and greatly expanded his deadly business.

Bad publicity drove Bout out of Belgium in 1997. He moved to the United Arab Emirates and continued business as usual, shipping weapons from Russia and Eastern Europe to a list of strife-torn nations that included Angola, Armenia, Cameroon, the Central African Republic, the Democratic Republic of the

Members of the Rendition Group follow a simple but standard procedure: Dressed head to toe in black, including masks, they blindfold and cut the clothes off their new captives, then administer an enema and sleeping drugs. They outfit detainees in a diaper and jumpsuit for what can be a day-long trip. Their destinations: either a detention facility operated by cooperative countries in the Middle East and Central Asia, including Afghanistan, or one of the CIA's own covert prisons—referred

Congo, Equatorial Guinea, Kenya, Liberia, Libya, the Republic of the Congo, Rwanda, Sierra Leone, South Africa, Sudan, Swaziland, and Uganda. Ignoring ideology, he sold weapons to anyone who had the cash on hand. Ironically, both the UN and the United States also hired Bout at various times, to arm "friendly" forces. Thus, Bout's second cargo airline, Air Cess, was established in Miami, Florida, in 1997.

Western authorities abandoned Bout in late 2001 over his ties to the terrorist group al-Qaeda. He fled to Russia in 2002 when Interpol, Belgian police, and the U.S. government issued warrants for his arrest. The UN froze his international bank accounts, but Russia's constitution bans extradition of its citizens to foreign nations. Bout might have been safe, but he could not resist the urge to travel and earn more money.

On March 1, 2008, Colombian authorities captured a laptop computer owned by members of a revolutionary group, the FARC. Information found on that computer revealed that Bout planned to sell the FARC a cache of arms, including military helicopters and 100 surface-to-air missiles used to destroy aircraft in flight. American DEA agents lured Bout to Bangkok, in a sting operation that climaxed with his arrest on March 6, 2008. His extradition trial began in Thailand on September 22, 2008, with attempts by Bout's attorney to dismiss charges of terrorist conspiracy. As yet, no resolution has been reached.

Bout's life inspired the 2005 film *Lord of War,* starring Nicholas Cage as fictional arms dealer "Yuri Orlov."

to in classified documents as "black sites," which at various times have been operated in eight countries, including several in Eastern Europe.[16]

Further investigation of "black sites" by the *Post* and the New York-based group Human Rights Watch prompted congressional calls for reform and full disclosure, while a defiant President Bush proclaimed that he felt no remorse for approving "enhanced interrogation techniques."[17]

PUNISHING INTERNATIONAL CRIME

Rendition aside, a legal mechanism exists for the arrest and international trial of certain offenders. In July 1998 representatives of 108 nations signed a treaty known as the Rome Statute, creating an International Criminal Court (ICC) to try offenders on various charges, including war crimes, genocide (defined as any acts "committed with intent to destroy, in whole or in part, a national, ethnical, racial or religious group, as such"), and crimes against humanity—a detailed list of acts (murder, rape, deportation, etc.) described as "particularly odious offences in that they constitute a serious attack on human dignity or grave humiliation or a degradation of one or more human beings." Although ratified in 1998, the Rome Statute did not take effect—and

PROJECT RECKONING

On September 17, 2008, U.S. Attorney General Michael Mukasey announced the arrest of 175 alleged drug traffickers in the United States and Italy. Aside from smuggling and selling cocaine and marijuana, the defendants also faced charges of attempted murder, conspiracy to kill and kidnap in a foreign country, solicitation and conspiracy to kidnap, conspiracy to use a firearm in a violent crime, interstate and foreign travel in aid of racketeering, money laundering, and other felonies.

The arrests were part of "Operation Reckoning," an international campaign involving the Justice Department's Special Operations Division, the DEA, FBI, IRS, U.S. Immigration and Customs Enforcement, and the U.S. Marshals Service. Aside from the feds, more than 200 state, local and foreign law enforcement agencies participated in the global investigation, through cooperation with the Washington-based Organized Crime Drug Enforcement Task Force. The September raids brought Operation Reckoning's total haul, over 15 months, to 507 arrests plus seizure of $60.1 million in cash, 176 vehicles, 167 weapons, 19 pounds of heroin, 1,039 pounds of methamphetamine, 36,764 pounds of cocaine, and 51,258 pounds of marijuana.[18]

the ICC was not convened—until July 2002.[19] Various nations that refused to sign the Rome Statute or to permit trial of their citizens before the ICC include China, India, and Russia. Israel and the United States signed in 1998, but renounced their approval in 2002, denying any future legal obligation to respect the court's rulings.

The ICC has proved to be a rather sluggish court. Between 2004 and 2007 it ordered four investigations of alleged crimes against humanity in the Democratic Republic of the Congo, Uganda, the Central African Republic, and Sudan.[20] Thus far, criminal charges have been filed against only one defendant, a Congolese soldier named Thomas Lubanga, accused of war crimes for drafting children to fight in the country's long civil war. Lubanga's trial began on January 26, 2009 and remained in progress as of late 2009.[21]

All of those arrested are alleged members of Mexico's Gulf Cartel, a drug syndicate based in Matamoros, just across the border from Brownsville, Texas. The cartel's elusive leaders are identified in federal incidements as Ezequiel Cardenas-Guillen, Heriberto Lazcano-Lazcano, and Jorge Eduardo Costilla-Sanchez. The gang ships huge amounts of drugs from Mexico, Colombia, Guatemala, and Panama to the United States and Europe, while "laundering" billions of dollars through various banks and legitimate businesses. Anyone competing with the gang is likely to be kidnapped, tortured, and killed.

While Attorney General Mukasey praised Operation Reckoning's success, echoed from Italy by anti-Mafia prosecutor Dr. Nicola Gratteri in Reggio Calabria, others admitted that the job was far from finished. David Nahmias, U.S. Attorney for the Northern District of Georgia, told reporters, "Metro Atlanta unfortunately continues to be a major drug distribution center for the Southeast and beyond. The DEA and our many other law enforcement partners continue to aggressively investigate all aspects of the drug trade." As long as Americans buy and use illegal drugs, that trade—and counterefforts like Operation Reckoning—will continue.

Helping
Ourselves

Skidmore, Missouri

Ken Rex McElroy was a bully. Born in 1934, he grew into a big, foul-tempered man who seemed to draw his greatest pleasure from abusing others. A lifelong thief and burglar, living on a farm outside Skidmore (population 450), he was indicted 22 times for various crimes but was convicted only once. Time after time McElroy terrorized his accusers and any witnesses who might testify against him. Once, when stopped by a highway patrolman on suspicion of raping a 12-year-old girl, McElroy threatened the officer with a shotgun, frightening him so badly that no charges were ever filed. Several other girls bore his children out of wedlock, and McElroy dodged another rape charge by marrying his 14-year-old victim in 1974.

Six years later, one of McElroy's sons fought with 70-year-old Bo Bowenkamp over a candy bar at a local grocery store. McElroy began stalking Bowenkamp, threatening him and finally blasting him with a shotgun. Bowenkamp survived his wounds and testified against McElroy in court, resulting in McElroy's first conviction, for attempted murder. Sadly for all concerned, McElroy filed an appeal and posted bail, resuming his harassment of Bowenkamp and menacing the jurors who convicted him.

On July 10, 1981, a group of Skidmore residents met with Nodaway County Sheriff Dan Estes to discuss McElroy's ongoing threats. Soon after Estes left town, McElroy arrived, brandishing guns on Main

Street and boasting of his plans for revenge against various enemies. A crowd gathered to listen, and then someone fired several shots, striking McElroy twice and killing him in the front seat of his pickup truck. By the time Sheriff Estes returned, the crowd had vanished. Trena McElroy identified her husband's alleged murderer as one Del Clement, but none of the 45 known witnesses admitted seeing anything, which left the crime officially unsolved. The minister who performed McElroy's funeral later fled town after receiving threats, and McElroy's widow soon followed. Arsonists burned McElroy's abandoned house in 1982.

In 1984 McElroy's widow filed a $5 million wrongful-death lawsuit against Sheriff Estes, Skidmore's mayor, and the alleged gunman Del Clement. The defendants settled out of court for $17,600, without admitting any guilt. The McElroy case recalled another crime in Nodaway County, dating from 1931, when local felon Raymond Gunn was shot before a crowd of some 3,000 people with no prosecution resulting.[1]

LYNCH LAW

From Colonial times through the 19th century, many American communities had no effective law enforcement apparatus. In some areas, police did not exist and circuit-riding judges only visited on rare occasions; other places had police and courts, but they were so corrupt or ineffective that criminals often escaped punishment. In those circumstances, "vigilance committees"—or vigilantes, for short—sometimes organized to dispose of lawbreakers without formal process of law. When threats, beatings, or tar-and-feather parties failed to do the job, lynch law prevailed.

Lynching—mob execution of alleged offenders without legal charges or trial—takes its name from Charles Lynch (1736–96), a Virginia planter and justice of the peace who directed mob violence against Tories (supporters of Britain) during America's Revolutionary War.[2] Over the next 175 years lynch mobs killed thousands of persons, many of whom were slain for their race, religion, or nationality, without any serious claims of criminal behavior. No definitive statistics are available, but Alabama's Tuskegee Institute counted 4,742 lynching victims (3,445 African Americans and 1,297 whites) between 1882 and 1951.[3] The last reported lynching in America occurred in June 1998, when white racists kidnapped victim James Byrd Jr. in Jasper, Texas, and dragged him for three miles behind their truck, resulting in Byrd's death.

While many lynchings were performed by local mobs, researchers have identified 326 organized vigilance committees active in 33 states between 1767 and 1902. Some, like South Carolina's Regulators (1767–69) and the San Francisco Committee of Vigilance, had thousands of members, but the majority claimed fewer than 100 active vigilantes. Few kept detailed records, since their actions were illegal, but a review of newspapers and other historical records reveals at least 729 persons executed. The true number is probably much higher.[4]

That tabulation does not include various Southern groups, led by the Ku Klux Klan (KKK) and Knights of the White Camellia, which were active during Reconstruction (1866–76). As usual, those groups claimed to be fighting crime, but most of their victims were newly freed slaves and white "radicals" who supported equal civil rights for African Americans. Again, no final tallies are available, but the KKK and its allied groups killed thousands of victims, while wounding, whipping, and otherwise torturing tens of thousands more. Between April and October 1868, racist vigilantes murdered 1,081 victims in Louisiana alone.[5]

Sadly, vigilante violence did not end with the dawn of the 20th century. World War I inspired new fears of "enemy aliens" and "subversives," while old-fashioned racism survived on both sides of the Mason-Dixon Line. The Ku Klux Klan revived in 1915, committing thousands of criminal attacks on racial and religious minorities, immigrants, labor unions, suspected Prohibition violators, and anyone else who offended the Klan's rigid sense of "morality." A second group—the American Legion, formed in 1919—also threatened, whipped, and occasionally murdered union leaders, antiwar protesters, and other "undesirables." Both the Klan and the Legion professed devotion to "100-percent Americanism"—a phrase coined by ex-president Theodore Roosevelt during World War I—but they reserved the sole right to decide who and what was "American."[6]

The national Klan dissolved in 1944, facing an IRS lien for unpaid taxes, then resurfaced in scattered fragments, resisting the advance of minority civil rights for another 30 years. The American Legion also calmed down after World War II, restricting its complaints to calls for censorship of "un-American" books, plays, and movies, but vigilante action continued in other forms. Rising crime rates and urban riots from 1964 to 1968 prompted the creation of local vigilance committees throughout the eastern United States, including some that carried guns and toured their districts in mock police cars. Some, like the White Hats of Cairo, Illinois, and the North Ward Citizens Committee of Newark, New Jersey, were openly racist and fraternized with the KKK. Cairo's vigilantes engaged in shootouts with African-American residents, and Cleveland's unofficial crime fighters were suspected (but never charged) in two unsolved 1968 murders. Most stopped short of violence, but their aggressive attitude did little to keep peace in troubled times.[7]

NEIGHBORHOOD WATCH

The Neighborhood Watch program, launched in 1972 by the National Sheriffs' Association (NSA), "counts on citizens to organize themselves and work with law enforcement to keep a trained eye and ear on their communities, while demonstrating their presence at all times of day and night." In 1982 the NSA released statistics claiming that 12 percent of all Americans were involved in local Neighborhood Watch programs, although the figures proved impossible to validate.[8]

Neighborhood Watch is not a vigilante group. It does not encourage members to pursue and capture criminals. Rather, members are instructed to rely on local police for enforcement, while recruiting local "window watchers," sponsoring crime- and drug-prevention programs in their communities, gathering criminal statistics on a local basis, assisting small businesses in repairing damaged or vandalized premises, and distributing literature on a wide range of subjects, including alcohol, tobacco and drugs, bullying, computer crimes, conflict resolution without violence, hate crimes, preparedness for disasters or terrorist attacks, plus school and workplace safety. While no reliable statistics are available, various Neighborhood Watch groups across the country claim credit for police captures of vandals, thieves, sexual predators, and other violent felons.

CRIME STOPPERS

Crime Stoppers began modestly in July 1976, following the hold-up-murder of college student Michael Carmen at a gas station in

SAN FRANCISCO COMMITTEE OF VIGILANCE

San Francisco residents organized their first vigilante group—variously called the Law and Order Party or the San Francisco Society of Regulators—in July 1849 to suppress a local gang of criminals known as the Hounds, who terrorized Mexican Americans. An estimated 100 men rallied to arrest the gang's leaders, who were subsequently indicted and legally convicted on charges of robbery, attempted murder, and conspiracy.

Three years later, in June 1851, crime rates in San Francisco proved distressing enough that a new Committee of Vigilance formed, claiming 700 members. The group hanged burglar John Jenkins (grand larceny was a capital crime in those days), followed by three more accused felons, and arrested 85 other suspects. Of those, one was publicly whipped, 14 were deported to Australia, 14 others were banished from California under threat of death, 15 were delivered to legal authorities for prosecution, and 41 were released without charges following investigation. The group officially dissolved in September 1851, although its leaders held private meetings over the next 18 months.[9]

In May 1856, following a political duel that left one man dead, the Committee of Vigilance was revived, claiming 6,000 members before it dissolved once again, three months later. Officially, the group hanged four more felons, but a fifth victim—professional boxer James "Yankee" Sullivan—committed suicide after being arrested and terrorized by committee members.

The new group sparked controversy with some of its actions, including its seizure of a federal arms shipment earmarked for California's state militia, and a mock trial staged against the chief justice of California's Supreme Court.

Albuquerque, New Mexico. When no witnesses came forward, Detective Greg MacAleese of the Albuquerque Police Department called upon his background as a former journalist, staging a televised re-

William Tecumseh Sherman, future Union hero of the Civil War, resigned his post as major-general of California's militia when Washington withdrew support from his campaign to crush the vigilantes. Sherman later wrote that the Committee of Vigilance "controlled the press, they wrote their own history, and the world generally gives them the credit of having purged San Francisco of rowdies and roughs; but their success has given great stimulus to a dangerous principle, that would at any time justify the mob in seizing all the power of government; and who is to say that the Vigilance Committee may not be composed of the worst, instead of the best, elements of a community? Indeed, in San Francisco, as soon as it was demonstrated that the real power had passed from the City Hall to the committee room, the same set of bailiffs, constables, and rowdies that had infested the City Hall were found in the employment of the 'Vigilantes.'"[10]

On the day they formally disbanded—August 11, 1856—San Francisco's vigilantes marched in a parade downtown to celebrate their supposed victory over crime. The group's passing did not end vigilante "justice" in the Golden State, however. Between 1856 and 1884, at least 26 other vigilance committees were identified in 19 California towns (three in Los Angeles, alone), claiming 54 identitifed victims.[11]

One who profited from joining the vigilantes was Leland Stanford (1824–93), an attorney and one of California's "Big Four" railroad barons, who organized the state's Republican Party during the same year he served on San Francisco's vigilance committee. Stanford's local popularity and wealth made him California's eighth governor (1862–63), and later a U.S. Senator (1885–93). In 1891 he donated $20 million to establish Stanford University, named in honor of son Leland Jr., who died from typhoid in 1884.

A Crime Stoppers billboard offers a cash reward for information on a wanted suspect. *AP Photo/Al Behrman*

creation of the slaying. The program brought a surprising response: within 72 hours, MacAleese had received multiple calls and identified the killers, charging two men with Carmen's murder and a string of previously unsolved robberies. More TV re-creations followed, formally organized under the Crime Stoppers logo, and Albuquerque witnessed a decline in crime that removed it from the list of America's 20 most dangerous cities.[12]

From those humble beginnings, Crime Stoppers spread nationwide (as Crime Stoppers USA), then circled the globe (as Crime Stoppers International). Today it operates in the United States, Canada, Bermuda, Great Britain, the Netherlands, Poland, Ukraine, South Africa, India, Australia, South Korea, and the Mariana Islands. Basic guidelines are the same in each location: Crime Stoppers films re-creations of various crimes, collaborating with local television stations, and offers cash rewards for information leading to arrest and conviction of the persons responsible.

The results, according to Crime Stoppers, are dramatic. In the United States, as of December 27, 2008, the group claims 806,163 crimes solved, with arrests of 476,947 defendants; $71,246,065 in rewards paid to informants; $1,036,683,323 worth of stolen property recovered; and seizure of drugs valued at $3,011,891,493. Worldwide, the statistics are even more impressive: 1,209,472 "cleared" cases, with 762,703 arrests; $89,512,248 paid out as rewards; $1,941,317,951 in stolen property recovered; and drugs seized with a retail value of $7,160,243,462.[13]

Aside from crime re-enactments, Crime Stoppers launched its first educational project in 1983, at a high school in Boulder, Colorado. Today, similar programs run year-round in more than 2,000 middle and high schools, junior colleges, and colleges from coast to coast. The programs cover campus crimes ranging from petty theft and vandalism to bullying, arson, bomb threats, and violent assaults. Cash rewards of $100 to $200 are offered in some schools for tips leading to confiscation of drugs or weapons, supplemented with free passes to various school activities or off-campus recreational facilities. Part of the goal is overcoming the negative connotation of "snitching," ingrained in some students from early childhood.[14]

Critics of Crime Stoppers warn that its informant program, which ensures the anonymity of those reporting crimes, may produce false accusations motivated by greed or personal spite. Police recognize that notorious crimes often serve as a vehicle for settling old grudges, and may attract mentally unbalanced individuals who claim responsibility for acts they did not commit. School-age children, some observers say, might even report nonexistent offenses for money or other rewards. Crime Stoppers administrators dismiss such concerns, insisting that all reports are fully investigated by proper authorities prior to filing of criminal charges or payment of any rewards.

POLICE ATHLETIC LEAGUES

Another approach to local crime fighting, with respect to young people and gangs, involves distracting potential offenders with sports or other recreational activities. New York City created the first Police Athletic League (PAL) in 1914, quickly expanding to six East Coast chapters. Today, operating as the National Association of Police Athletics/Activities

Leagues, 350 PAL chapters nationwide serve an estimated 2 million young people, ranging between the ages of five and 18. Sponsored events include three national amateur boxing contests, wherein contestants may win places on the U.S. Olympic Boxing Team; baseball competitions, including the Annual Junior Olympic Championships and participation by 125 youths in Japan's yearly World Children's Baseball Fair; team sports supported by the National Football League, National Hockey League, National Basketball Association, and National Women's Basketball Association; and a Golf Challenge League supported by the U.S. Golf Association, with the stated goal to "hook a kid on golf."[15]

Aside from traditional sports, PAL educates young participants on the dangers of crime and strives in other ways to prepare them for adult life. The Court TV network provides its "Choices & Consequences" video and lesson plans to PAL chapters nationwide. PAL's Trips for Kids program furnishes mountain bikes and offers participants their first glimpse of America beyond their urban neighborhoods. Other programs help PAL members with homework and other school activities. While it is difficult, if not impossible, to judge the impact of such programs, PAL describes itself as:

> a youth crime prevention program that utilizes educational, athletic, and recreational activities to create trust and understanding between police officers and youth. It is based on the conviction that young people—if they are reached early enough—can develop strong positive attitudes toward police officers in their journey through life toward the goal of maturity and good citizenship. The PAL program brings youth under the supervision and positive influence of a law enforcement agency and expands public awareness about the role of a police officer and the reinforcement of the responsible values and attitudes instilled in young people by their parents. Studies have shown that if a young person respects a police officer on the ball field, gym or classroom, the youth will likely come to respect the laws that police officers enforce. Such respect is beneficial to the youth, the police officer, the neighborhood and the business community.[16]

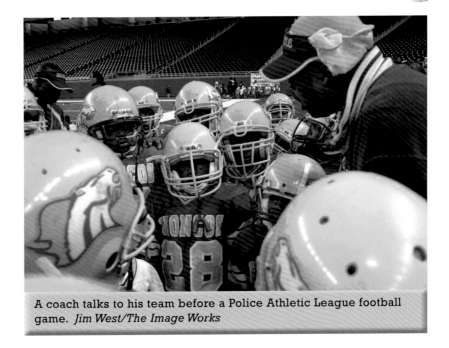

A coach talks to his team before a Police Athletic League football game. *Jim West/The Image Works*

GETTING MADD

Mothers Against Drunk Driving (MADD) had very different origins and goals. Candace Lightner launched the group in 1980, after a drunken hit-and-run driver killed her 13-year-old daughter near their home in Fair Oaks, California. While limited at first to local efforts, MADD grew swiftly after *MADD*, a made-for-TV movie, received two Emmy nominations in 1983. Today, the organization has 304 active chapters nationwide.[17]

MADD's first national ally was New Jersey Senator Frank Lautenberg, who noted that teens banned from drinking in his state could legally buy alcohol in New York. Lautenberg sponsored the 1984 National Minimum Drinking Age Act, which reduced federal highway funds for states that allowed persons under 21 to buy liquor. While some states resisted raising their minimum drinking ages, all finally complied after the U.S. Supreme Court upheld the law in 1987. MADD received another unwelcome boost from tragedy in May 1988 when a drunk driver hit a Kentucky school bus, killing 27 persons and injuring 34 others.

MADD's earliest campaigns sought stricter punishment of drunken drivers, when many jurisdictions imposed only small fines or probation. Many new laws have been passed nationwide since the group's creation, increasing penalties for both first-time and repeat offenders.

GUARDIAN ANGELS

Curtis Sliwa, a Brooklyn native born in 1954, tried a new approach to neighborhood crime fighting in February 1979. With a dozen friends, he formed the "Magnificent 13," an unarmed group trained in martial arts created to ride New York's subways and arrest any violent criminals they encountered. (Any person in America may make a "citizen's arrest," while risking lawsuits or criminal charges if an innocent person is arrested or a suspect's civil rights are violated in the process.) As the group attracted new recruits, Sliwa changed its name to the Guardian Angels, adopting red berets and printed shirts or jackets as a standard uniform. Patrols spread from the subways to crime-ridden streets and housing projects, overcoming early official resistance to win praise from New York mayors Ed Koch, Rudolph Giuliani, and Michael Bloomberg.

Today, aside from New York, the Alliance of Guardian Angels has active chapters in 88 cities, spanning 30 states. Outside of the United States, chapters operate in eight Canadian cities (despite public opposition from Toronto's mayor and police chief); in Mexico City; in Rio de Janeiro, Brazil; in Peru (three chapters); in London; in Denmark (seven chapters); in Israel; in Italy; in South Africa (three chapters); in Australia (two chapters); in New Zealand (three chapters); in the Philippines (two chapters); and in Japan (24 chapters).[18]

Six Guardian Angels have died "on duty" since the group was organized. Malcolm Brown was shot by a still-unidentified New York mugger on July 3, 1981. A Newark policeman shot Frank Melvin on December 30, 1981, apparently mistaking him for a gang member. (Police initially claimed Melvin was

MADD also lobbied for change in the level of blood-alcohol concentration (BAC) used to calculate legal intoxication, resulting in passage of a federal law in 2000 that changed the legal maximum from .10 to .08. By 2005, all 50 states and the District of Columbia had changed their

shot by a rooftop sniper, but then said he had approached the officer's patrol car "in a hostile manner." No charges were filed.) Members of a Bronx street gang shot Juan Olivia on July 30, 1983, leaving him in a coma until he died on Christmas Day. A supermarket burglar stabbed Sherman Geiger in Yonkers, New York, on August 24, 1987. Glen Doser suffered fatal gunshot wounds when he stopped two men from robbing a Los Angeles woman on March 18, 1993. James Richards was shot by unknown gunmen outside his home on October 18, 2000, during a campaign to rid his L.A. neighborhood of crime and drugs.[19]

A relatively new branch of the Guardian Angels, dubbed CyberAngels, premiered in 1995 to monitor Internet chat rooms in search of sexual predators. From that modest beginning the program has expanded to become "a virtual learning community," collaborating with school boards in New York and New Jersey on a series of classroom presentations involving such issues as gangs, bullying, and cyberstalking. The CyberAngels Learning Center offers tips on subjects ranging from selection of an Internet service provider, computer terminology and mechanical problems, to broader issues of personal security. In 1998 President Bill Clinton honored CyberAngels with a President's Service Award. The following year, New York City Mayor Rudolph Giuliani saluted the program by declaring "Guardian Angels Day," in recognition of the CyberAngels unit's work online. In October 2006 New York Governor George Pataki announced the start of formal collaboration between CyberAngels and the New York State Office of Cyber Security & Critical Infrastructure, working toward improved computer-safety education for the state's teachers, students, and parents.[20]

laws accordingly. MADD spokesmen note that while overall highway traffic deaths increased from 56,209 in 1982 to 59,104 in 2005, alcohol-related fatalities declined from 19,610 in 1982 to 11,820 during the same period.[21]

Since 1999 MADD's focus has expanded to include campaigns against underage drinking and calls for an increase in beer excise taxes to equal the tax on hard liquor. In April 2008 MADD spokesmen condemned the video game *Grand Theft Auto IV* for glamorizing auto theft and reckless driving. Some civil libertarians complain that MADD's campaigns have prompted police to establish random highway sobriety checkpoints, which amount to illegal searches without warrants. MADD's leaders reply that "opponents of sobriety checkpoints tend to be those who drink and drive frequently and are concerned about being caught."[22]

8

Crime and the Media

Tulsa, Oklahoma

Around 4:00 P.M. on May 30, 1921, 19-year-old Dick Rowland boarded an elevator occupied by 17-year-old Sarah Page, in Tulsa's Drexel Building. Rowland, an African American, was on his way to use the building's "colored" restroom. Page, the building's elevator operator, was white.

Stories differ radically about what happened next. Some say that Rowland tripped on the elevator's threshold and grabbed Page's arm to keep from falling. Others claim the couple knew each other and resumed an old quarrel upon meeting by chance. A clerk from a shop on the building's first floor allegedly heard Page cry out and ran to her aid, then assumed the worst and summoned police, who took Rowland into custody. Officers questioned Page, but kept no record of her statement. Before police could finish their investigation, the *Tulsa Tribune* ran a story with the headline: "Nab Negro for Attacking Girl in Elevator." A front-page editorial reported that local whites planned "To Lynch Negro Tonight."[1]

It was no idle threat. In 1921, and for years thereafter, Tulsa was dominated by racists who joined the Ku Klux Klan in large numbers. Any threat, real or imaginary, from African Americans might provoke a violent reaction. On May 31 when police charged Rowland with assault—a frequent euphemism for attempted rape in those days— residents of Tulsa's Greenwood ghetto feared a lynching might result. By 10:30 P.M. an estimated 1,500 African Americans had gathered at the Tulsa courthouse, some of them with weapons. A white civilian tried to seize one black man's pistol and a shot rang out, followed by an exchange of gunfire that wounded a dozen people.[2]

What followed is remembered as the "Tulsa Race War," a 16-hour riot that left the Greenwood district in ashes, with an uncertain number of persons killed and injured. Sheriff Willard McCullough saved Dick Rowland from lynching, but wild rumors inflated by the *Tulsa Tribune* and competing *Tulsa World* drove Klansmen and other white racists into a murderous frenzy. City police, state troopers, National Guardsmen, and members of the local American Legion often appeared to side with white rioters, including confused reports that airplanes from nearby Curtis Field were dropping bombs over Greenwood.

Whatever the truth of those stories, confusion still surrounds the final toll of death and destruction in Tulsa. Official reports list 36 dead—26 African Americans and 10 whites. Other published stories cite body counts ranging from 77 to 300, with the majority of victims in each case described as African Americans. Red Cross spokesmen stated that 531 persons received first-aid treatment during the riot, while 346 African Americans required surgery (with 82 cases listed as "major" operations). Estimates of property destroyed—nearly all of it owned by African Americans—ranged from $750,000 to $1.5 million. Red Cross observers counted 1,115 homes destroyed, with another 314 looted but left standing. African-American victims filed more than 1,400 lawsuits against Tulsa officials, citing police negligence for losses exceeding $4 million, but no record on the disposition of those cases has survived.[3]

Today, historians agree that racist articles and editorials in Tulsa's newspapers inflamed the mob that rampaged through Greenwood, killing and burning. Some believe no riot would have happened, if the *World* and *Tribune* had not tried to boost their sales by pandering to hatred and extremism.

GLORIFYING CRIME

Complaints of journalists contributing to crime did not begin in 1921. For half a century beforehand, sensational (and largely fictitious) "dime novels" had chronicled the lives of Western lawmen, gunfighters, and outlaws, frequently inventing "facts" to glorify cold-blooded killers such as Billy the Kid or Jesse James and the Younger brothers. Sales were all that mattered, and some of the fantasies published for profit now pass as "history" in the minds of many Americans.

A similar phenomenon occurred during Prohibition and the Great Depression. First came flamboyant bootleggers like Al Capone, Dutch Schultz, and "Bugsy" Siegel, fighting turf wars and corrupting the authorities, while newspapers eagerly followed their exploits. Many readers viewed the gang wars as a form of public entertainment, unwisely taking Siegel at his word when he said, "We [gangsters] only kill each other."[4] Around the time of Prohibition's repeal in 1933 a new collection of flamboyant outlaws appeared, robbing banks and kidnapping rich men for ransom. Millions of Americans, jobless and homeless since the Wall Street crash of 1929, cheered bandits who attacked public symbols of corporate greed. A few such thieves, like Oklahoma's "Pretty Boy" Floyd, burned mortgage papers during bank holdups, thus expanding their public support.

Complaints of the media glorifying crime continue to the present day. An anonymous quotation, "If it bleeds, it leads," is often used to characterize television news broadcasts focused on violent crime, gruesome accidents, and natural disasters.[5] In response to such criticism, many TV stations and newspapers now strive to include "happy-ending" stories, but the public appetite for crime and violence appears to be insatiable.

A SOUNDING BOARD FOR PSYCHOS?

Some violent offenders seem driven to communicate with the media. Jesse James once wrote his own press release and left it at a robbery scene in Missouri. In the 1930s bandits John Dillinger, Clyde Barrow, and Pretty Boy Floyd all wrote letters to local newspapers. However, such communications seem most common in cases involving serial killers.

London police received hundreds of letters during their search for "Jack the Ripper," a still-unidentified slayer who claimed five victims during 1888. The killer himself—or a hoaxer—coined the famous nickname that has inspired countless books, films and plays over the past 120-plus years. While some of the Ripper notes included details of the crimes, and one came with a partial human kidney, experts disagree on whether any of the letters originated from Jack. Some feel that all were written by reporters, pranksters, or mentally ill individuals seeking a moment in the spotlight, but the notes inspired panic and still fuel ongoing debates.

Another unidentified killer, the "Axeman of New Orleans," killed seven victims and wounded five others during a series of home invasions between May 1918 and October 1919. The killer, or someone else, also taunted police with various letters during the crime spree. One note, published in local newspapers on March 13, 1919, threatened death to anyone who did not play jazz music on St. Joseph's Night (March 19). That night, loud music played throughout New Orleans, and no attacks occurred.

George Metesky (1903–94), better known as New York City's "Mad Bomber," planted 33 bombs around town between 1940 and 1956, injuring 15 victims in 22 explosions. (The other bombs were duds.)[6] Between bombings, Metesky sent notes to the New York Police Department, the *New York Herald Tribune,* and the *New York Journal American,* including demands for "justice" against the Consolidated Edison Company. Detectives eventually traced Metesky, a former Con Ed employee who blamed the company for an illness that forced his premature retirement, and arrested him in January 1957. A court committed Metesky to Matteawan State Hospital, where he remained until 1973.

Yet another unidentified serial killer, California's "Zodiac," coined his own media nickname in a series of letters to police, newspapers, and TV stations, written between 1968 and 1970. Unlike the Ripper notes from London, much of the information contained in Zodiac's letters had not been released to the media, and he enclosed pieces of one victim's bloody shirt in letters received on October 14 and December 20, 1969. As in the Ripper's case, speculation over suspects and motives continues to the present day.

Dennis Lynn Rader killed 10 victims in and around Wichita, Kansas, between 1974 and 1991, mailing several letters signed "BTK"—for "Bind, Torture and Kill"—to police, the *Wichita Eagle* and local television stations. Rader's last communication was received on February 16, 2005, nine days before police finally identified him with the aid of family members. Rader confessed his crimes in custody and received 10 consecutive life sentences in August 2005.

Convicted serial killer Dennis Rader, known as the BTK Strangler, walks into the El Dorado Correctional Facility with two sheriff's officers. Rader mailed several letters to police, local television stations, and the *Wichita Eagle* before being apprehended in February 2005. *Jeff Tuttle/epa/Corbis*

In February 1974 members of an extremist group called the Symbionese Liberation Army (SLA) kidnapped newspaper heiress Patricia Hearst in Berkeley, California. First, the SLA demanded freedom for two members accused of murdering Oakland's school superintendent, but when police refused the group ordered distribution of free food to local poor people. While Hearst's family complied, she sent audio tapes to the media, condemning her wealthy parents and America's "fascist" government. In April 1974 bank security cameras caught Hearst carrying a rifle during a $10,000 robbery. Four SLA members died in a shootout with Los Angeles Police Department the following month, and FBI agents captured Hearst in September 1975. Despite claims of brainwashing and torture, jurors convicted her of robbery and she served 21 months in prison.

While British police hunted the "Yorkshire Ripper" during 1975-80, they received three letters and an audio tape from someone claiming to be the killer. Suspect Peter Sutcliffe later confessed to 13 murders and received a life sentence, but police admitted that he had not mailed the tape or letters. Officers dismissed the correspondence as a hoax, but author David Yallop, in his book *Deliver Us from Evil* (1981), suggests that the still-unknown writer may be responsible for several other slayings.

"Stocking Strangler" Carlton Gary terrorized Columbus, Georgia, during 1977-78, murdering seven elderly women in their homes. Before his arrest, another slayer killed two African-American women in Columbus and sent a letter to police claiming the victims were killed in retaliation for the strangler's murders of white women. Suspect William Hance—himself an African American—was later convicted of those slayings and executed in 1994. Gary received a life sentence for his crimes.

Echoes of George Metesky surfaced in the case of Theodore Kaczynski, dubbed the "Unabomber" by FBI agents because some of the 16 bombs he mailed or planted between 1978 and 1995 exploded at universities. The blasts killed three victims and wounded 21 others.[7] In April 1995 Kaczynski wrote to the *New York Times,* promising no further bombings if newspapers would print a 35,000-word "manifesto" on industrial society. The *Times* and *Washington Post* published the document five months later, despite widespread criticism. G-men arrested Kaczynski in April 1996, and he received a life sentence in January 1998.

DOES THE MEDIA "CAUSE" CRIME?

Some critics blame the news and entertainment media for more than simply glamorizing criminals or giving lunatics a public forum. Others claim the media actually causes crime, either by prompting imitation of fictional and real-life felonies, or by desensitizing viewers—especially young people—to the point where violence seems normal and "fun." In a few cases, media figures have even been accused of "brainwashing" teenagers to commit violent acts.

Imitative (or "copycat") crimes do occur, and some apparently mimic portrayals of fictional crimes in films or on television. Actors in the movie *Fuzz* (1972) set fire to homeless men, allegedly prompting some real-life Boston youths to do the same thing. After shooting President Ronald Reagan in 1981, John Hinckley claimed he did it to impress actress Jodie Foster, whose performance in the 1976 film *Taxi Driver* (including a botched political assassination) obsessed Hinckley. Despite such claims, research has shown that most copycat felons have criminal records before they decide to imitate events lifted from fiction or current events.[8]

Can music "cause" crime? John McCollum's parents thought so, when he shot himself in 1984 while listening to Ozzy Osbourne's song "Suicide Solution." A court dismissed their lawsuit against Osbourne in 1986, and similar lawsuits filed by two other grieving families were likewise thrown out, but complaints continued. Canadian killer James Jollimore claimed that he stabbed three people while under the influence of Osbourne's song "Bark at the Moon." Most psychologists dismiss such claims, noting that song lyrics are taken out of context to "prove" the complaints, while 306 classic operas depict 77 suicides—far more than any modern rock or heavy metal tunes—without provoking similar reactions.[9]

MOST WANTED

Despite frequent criticism, the media also helps catch criminals. The organization Crime Stoppers re-enacts crimes on TV to spark the memory of witnesses, and many law enforcement agencies also use the media directly in their search for fugitives at large.

In 1949 reporter William Hutchinson asked J. Edgar Hoover for a list of the "toughest guys" sought by the FBI. The resultant newspaper article produced so much positive feedback that Hoover created the FBI's "Ten Most Wanted" list in March 1950, broadcasting photographs and brief case histories of major fugitives across the country and around the world. Since then the list has featured 491 subjects, 460 of whom have been captured, including 151 located through tips from the public.[10]

"SON OF SAM"

Between July 1976 and July 1977 residents of New York City were terrorized by an elusive gunman who killed six victims and wounded nine more in eight random shootings. The same pistol was used in all eight attacks, prompting reporters to dub New York's gunman the ".44-Caliber Killer." Panic increased, however, when the shooter left a letter at the scene of his fifth attack, in April 1977, and gave himself a new nickname. That letter, addressed to the NYPD, read:

> Dear Captain Joseph Borrelli,
> I am deeply hurt by your calling me a wemon [*sic*] hater! I am not. But I am a monster. I am the "Son of Sam." I am a little brat. When father Sam gets drunk he gets mean. He beats his family. Sometimes he ties me up to the back of the house. Other times he locks me in the garage. Sam loves to drink blood. "Go out and kill," commands father Sam. Behind our house some rest. Mostly young—raped and slaughtered—their blood drained—just bones now. Papa Sam keeps me locked in the attic too. I can't get out but I look out the attic window and watch the world go by. I feel like an outsider. I am on a different wavelength then [*sic*] everybody else—programmed too [*sic*] kill. However, to stop me you must kill me. Attention all police: Shoot me first—shoot to kill or else keep out of my way or you will die! Papa Sam is old now. He needs some blood to preserve his youth. He has had too many heart attacks. "Ugh, me hoot, it hurts, sonny boy." I miss my pretty princess most of all. She's resting in our ladies house. But I'll see her soon. I am the "Monster"—"Beelzebub"—the chubby behemouth. I love to hunt. Prowling the streets looking for fair game—tasty meat. The wemon of Queens

Criteria for choosing the FBI's Ten Most Wanted has changed over time. The early lists focused on traditional murderers, bandits, and kidnappers, shifting toward black militants and antiwar radicals in the

are prettyist [*sic*] of all. It must be the water they drink. I live for the hunt—my life. Blood for papa. Mr. Borrelli, sir, I don't want to kill anymore. No sur [*sic*], no more but I must, "honor thy father." I want to make love to the world. I love people. I don't belong on earth. Return me to yahoos. To the people of Queens, I love you. And I want to wish all of you a happy Easter. May God bless you in this life and in the next. And for now I say goodbye and goodnight. Police: Let me haunt you with these words: I'll be back! I'll be back! To be interpreted as—bang bang bang, bank [*sic*], bang—ugh!! Yours in murder, Mr. Monster.[11]

The .44-Caliber Killer thus became "Son of Sam."

A parking ticket from the final crime scene led police to suspect David Berkowitz on August 9, 1977. Officers found the murder weapon in his possession, and Berkowitz admitted the killings, initially claiming that he took orders from a dog owned by neighbor Sam Carr—the "Papa Sam" of his letter. Later, Berkowitz dropped his insanity plea and pled guilty in court, receiving six life prison terms.

Later still, Berkowitz confused matters by claiming that some of the murders were committed by a Satanic cult, whose membership included two sons of Sam Carr (both deceased by that time). Most authorities dismissed those claims, but journalist Maury Terry presented some apparent supporting evidence in his book *The Ultimate Evil* (1987). That evidence included Berkowtiz's knowledge of an unsolved 1974 ritual murder in California, allegedly committed by suspect William Mentzer, whom Berkowitz identified as an associate of 1960s cult killer Charles Manson. Though never charged in that case, Mentzer received a life sentence for the 1983 slaying of Hollywood movie producer Roy Radin.

JOHN EMIL LIST (1925–2008)

John List appeared to be the very image of respectability. A son of German immigrants, he served in the Pacific with the U.S. Army during World War II, and then earned a master's degree in accounting from the University of Michigan. In private life he was married with three children, a devout Lutheran Sunday-school teacher in Westfield, New Jersey. He also had a darker side, however, indicated by his frequent loss of jobs and mounting debts, which seemed impossible to pay.

On November 11, 1971, the dark side won out. After his children left for school, List shot his wife Helen at the breakfast table, then went upstairs and killed his 84-year-old mother in her attic bedroom. That afternoon, he drove 16-year-old daughter Patricia home from school and killed her, then repeated the process with 13-year-old son Frederick. John Jr., age 15, came home alone and was the last to die, shot 10 times at close range. His bloody work complete, List ate dinner and went to bed, delaying his flight from Westfield until the next morning.

List's neighbors did not hear the gunshots, and his family had maintained such strict privacy that no one missed them for a month. His children's teachers believed the notes that List mailed before fleeing, claiming that his family had to spend several weeks in North Carolina. By the time the murders were discovered, John List had vanished.

He would not be seen again—at least, under that name—for 18 years.

late 1960s and early 1970s, then changing again to include members of organized crime and serial killers after Hoover's death in 1972. At the time of this writing, the current list included terrorist leader Osama bin Laden, Boston mobster James "Whitey" Bulger, four other killers with eight victims between them, one child molester, one escaped convict, and a gunman sought for wounding a police officer. The 10th fugitive,

In 1989 New Jersey homicide detectives approached the producers of *America's Most Wanted,* requesting help with their state's most famous case since the Lindbergh kidnapping of 1932. (Unknown to police and *AMW* host John Walsh, List himself was a fan of the show, later admitting that he wondered if his case would rate profiling on the program.) In preparation for the broadcast, *AMW* hired forensic sculptor Frank Bender to study photographs of List and prepare a clay bust of the fugitive as he might look at age 64. List's story and Bender's likeness of the fugitive aired on May 21, 1989, resulting in more than 200 telephone tips from viewers around the country, ranging from Denver, Colorado, to Richmond, Virginia—where one lead finally paid off.[12]

After fleeing New Jersey, List had lived in Denver and in Midlothian, Virginia, before finally settling in Richmond as "Robert Peter Clark"—a name borrowed from a former college classmate who could not remember meeting List in person. FBI agents arrested List at work on June 1, 1989, and while he denied his true identity, fingerprints soon revealed his lie. On April 12, 1990, jurors convicted List on five counts of first-degree murder. He received five consecutive life sentences on May 1.

Interviewed by reporter Connie Chung in February 2002, List cited Bible texts to justify the murders of his family and claim that he had been forgiven for his crimes. He had not killed himself in 1971, List said, because suicide was a mortal sin and it would have kept him from joining his loved ones in heaven. List died in prison on March 21, 2008, without ever expressing remorse for the slaughter of his family.

Victor Gerena, has been on the list since 1983, sought for a $7 million holdup in Connecticut.

The FBI's Top Ten fugitives are not prioritized—there is no "Number 1" on the Most Wanted list. Selection is theoretically made based on the threat a fugitive poses to society and on the estimated value of publicizing his or her case. Eight women made the list between 1968 and 2007, but Patricia Hearst (see above) was not listed in 1974-75 because her case attracted international publicity without placing her name on the Top Ten roster.

The FBI's Most Wanted list proved so successful that other agencies soon created their own dishonor rolls, in a bid to share the publicity. The U.S. Marshals Service established its "15 Most Wanted" list in 1983, in what agency spokesmen called "an effort to prioritize the investigation and apprehension of high-profile offenders who are considered to be some of the country's most dangerous fugitives."[13] Other federal agencies with "most wanted" lists posted on the Internet include the ATF, DEA, the Secret Service, U.S. Immigration and Customs Enforcement, and the U.S. Postal Inspection Service. Nationwide at least 40 state police agencies post lists of fugitives online, as do many local police and sheriff's departments.[14]

In July 1981 a serial killer kidnapped and murdered six-year-old Adam Walsh in Hollywood, Florida. That personal tragedy drove Adam's father, John Walsh, to become a crusader for missing and victimized children, later expanding his focus to include pursuit of dangerous felons nationwide. On February 7, 1988, the Fox television network premiered *America's Most Wanted*, with Walsh as the program's host. *AMW* profiles criminal cases with suspects at large, broadcasts their photographs in cases where the fugitives have been identified, and invites viewers to contact law enforcement agencies with any information they possess that may assist police in capturing the suspects.

America's Most Wanted scored its first victory four days after the first episode aired—on February 11, 1988—with the arrest of triple-killer David James Roberts in New York. (Roberts was also on the FBI's Most Wanted list.) On December 23, 2008, LAPD officers shot and killed *AMW*'s 1,052nd fugitive, former child-actor Mark Everett, wanted for murdering his ex-girlfriend and kidnapping their son in Hawthorne, California.[15]

AMW's success rate—contributing to the arrest of one fugitive per week for 20 years—has created a broad base of loyal fans. The show was Fox's first hit program, and today it is the network's longest-running show. When network executives canceled *AMW* in 1996, protests from viewers, police, and public officials—including 37 state governors and

John Walsh hosts the television show *America's Most Wanted*, which has aided in the apprehension of over 1,000 fugitives since it premiered in February 1988. *AP Photo/Reed Saxon*

55 members of Congress—forced Fox to resume broadcasting the series six weeks later. Local Fox affiliate stations also air local "most wanted" programs in 37 major cities nationwide.[16]

Endnotes

Introduction

1. BrainyQuote, "Lucius Annaeus Seneca quotes," http://www. brainyquote.com/quotes/quotes/l/ q122586.html (Accessed October 15, 2009); Laurence Peter, *Peter's Quotations* (New York: Bantam, 1979), 126.

2. World of Quotes, "Henry Thomas Buckle quotes," http://www. worldofquotes.com/author/Henry-Thomas-Buckle/1/index.html (Accessed October 15, 2009); Peter, 127.

3. Robert F. Kennedy, "On the Mindless Menace of Violence," Robert F. Kennedy Memorial, http:// www.rfkmemorial.org/lifevision/ onthemindlessmenaceofviolence (Accessed October 15, 2009).

Chapter 1

1. William Branigin, "FBI Agent Dies Raiding Home of Suspected Cocaine Dealer," *Washington Post,* November 20, 2008.

2. U.S. Department of Justice, "DEA Nets Largest Meth Seizure Ever in New Jersey," Drug Enforcement Administration press release, http://www.usdoj.gov/dea/pubs/ states/newsrel/2008/nwk120208. html (Accessed October 15, 2009.)

3. Val Walton, "Birmingham Mayor Larry Langford Indicted," *Birmingham News*, December 2, 2008.

4. Federal Bureau of Investigation, "FBI Uniform Crime Reports, 2008" http://www.fbi.gov/ucr/ cius2008/index.html (Accessed October 15, 2009).

5. "FBI Uniform Crime Reports 2008."

6. "FBI Uniform Crime Reports 2008"; "Active U.S. Hate Groups," Southern Poverty Law Center, http://www.splcenter.org/intel/ map/hate.jsp (Accessed October 15, 2009).

7. Federal Bureau of Investigation, "Financial Crimes Report to the Public Fiscal Year 2007," http://www.fbi.gov/publications/ financial/fcs_report2007/ financial_crime_2007.htm (Accessed June 21, 2008).

8. U.S. Department of Justice, "DEA Stats & Facts," http://www.usdoj. gov/dea/statistics.html (Accessed June 21, 2008).

9. Bureau of Justice Statistics, "Law Enforcement Statistics," http:// www.ojp.usdoj.gov/bjs/lawenf.htm (Accessed June 21, 2008).

10. North Central State College (Mansfield, OH), "Weird American Sex Laws," http://www. ncstatecollege.edu/Webpub/

Blewis/ Acrobatfiles/sexlaws.pdf (Accessed June 21, 2008).

11. Officer.com, "The Directory," http://www.officer.com/links/ Agency_Search (Accessed June 21, 2008).

12. Gambling Laws U.S., http://www. gambling-law-us.com (Accessed June 21, 2008); *Cape Cod Times*, "U.S. Gambling Timeline," July 24, 1977.

13. Sex Laws, http://www.geocities. com/CapitolHill/2269/?20086 (Accessed June 21, 2008).

14. Alcohol Problems and Solutions, "Alcohol and Drinking Facts in States across the US," http://www2. potsdam.edu/hansondj/funfacts/ FactsByState.html (Accessed June 21, 2008).

15. Marianne W. Zawitz, "Guns Used in Crime," Bureau of Justice Statistics, http://www.ojp.usdoj.gov/ bjs/pub/pdf/guic.pdf (Accessed June 21, 2008); Public Broadcasting Station, "Gun Stats and Facts," http://www.pbs.org/wgbh/pages/ frontline/shows/guns/more/facts. html (Accessed June 21, 2008).

16. Bureau of Labor Statistics, "Census of Fatal Occupational Injuries," http://www.bls.gov/ iif/oshwc/cfoi/cftb0223.pdf (Accessed June 21, 2008); Officer Down Memorial Page, "Honoring Officers Killed in the Year 2007," http://www.odmp.org/ year.php?year=2007&Submit=Go (Accessed June 21, 2008).

17. Vincent Sacco, *When Crime Waves* (Thousand Oaks, Calif.: Sage, 2005), 1–5.

18. National Law Enforcement Officers Memorial Fund, "A Walking Tour of the Memorial," http://

www.nleomf.com/TheMemorial/ walktour.htm (Accessed June 21, 2008); "FBI Uniform Crime Reports 2007."

19. William Helmer and Rick Mattix, *Public Enemies* (New York: Checkmark, 1998), 292–303.

20. Federal Bureau of Investigation, FBI Press Release, July 28, 2008, http://www.fbi.gov/pressrel/ pressrel08/bankstats072808.htm (Accessed October 16, 2009).

21. Anthony Summers, *The Arrogance of Power* (New York: Viking, 2000), 54–7, 118–24, 465–86.

22. Officer Down Memorial Page, http://www.odmp.org/browse.php.

23. Texas Ranger Hall of Fame, "Francis Augustus Hamer," http:// www.texasranger.org/halloffame/ Hamer_Frank.htm (Accessed June 21, 2008); John Kobler, *Ardent Spirits* (New York: G. P. Putnam's Sons, 1973), 293; David Chalmers, *Hooded Americanism* (Chicago: Quadrangle, 1968), 331.

24. Bureau of Justice Stats, "Policing and Homicide, 1976-98," http:// www.ojp.usdoj.gov/bjs/pub/pdf/ ph98.pdf (Accessed June 21, 2008).

25. Fox Butterfield, "When Police Shoot, Who's Counting?" *New York Times,* April 29, 2001; Lynn Hulsey, "Cincinnati Tops List of Police Killings of Blacks," *Dayton Daily News*, April 28, 2001; Roger Roy, "Killings by Police Under-Reported," *Orlando Sentinel,* May 24, 2004; Rick Hepp, "Most NJ Police Shooting Targets Were Minorities in '07," *Newark Star-Ledger*, December 9, 2007; "Death by Police Shooting," Inquest, http://inquest.gn.apc.org/

data_death_by_police_shooting.
html (Accessed June 21, 2008).

Chapter 2

1. International World History Project, "The Reforms of Uurukagina,"
http://history-world.org/reforms_
of_urukagina.htm (June 23, 2008).
2. Capital Punishment U.K., "History
of the Death Penalty in Britain,"
http://www.capitalpunishmentuk.
org/contents.html (Accessed June
23, 2008).
3. U.S. Constitution, amend. 8.
4. Carla Hesse, "The Law of the Terror," *MLN* 114, 4 (September 1999):
702–18.
5. J.J. Finkelstein, "The Laws of Ur-
Nammu," *Journal of Cuneiform
Studies* 22, 3/4 (1968–69): 66–82.
6. Bill O'Neal, *The Pimlico Encyclopedia of Western Gunfighters* (London: Pimlico, 1998), 22, 96–103,
134–39, 302–5.
7. Online Etymology Dictionary,
"Racket," http://www.etymonline.
com/index.php?term=racket
(Accessed June 23, 2008).
8. Alain Sanders and Priscilla Pain-
ton, "Law: Showdown at Gucci,"
Time, August 21, 1989, http://
www.time.com/time/magazine/
article/0,9171,958402-1,00.html
(Accessed June 23, 2008).
9. Arthur Rotstein, "Border Patrol
Horses Get Special Feed that
Helps Protect Desert Ecosystem,"
Associated Press, June 9, 2005,
http://enn.com/top_stories/
article/1731 (Accessed June 23,
2008)
10. Kent Police Museum, "History,"
http://www.kent-police-museum.
co.uk/core_pages/history.shtml
(Accessed June 23, 2008).
11. Akron and Summit County
History, "Police," http://www.
akronhistory.org/police.htm
(Accessed June 23, 2008).
12. Rita Ciolli, "Verdict Rekindles
Debate over Racketeering Law,"
Newsday, December 12, 1988.

Chapter 3

1. Officer Down Memorial Page,
"Honoring All Fallen Members of
the New Orleans Police Department," http://www.odmp.org/
agency/2748-new-orleans-police-
department-louisiana (Accessed
June 23, 2008).
2. Los Angeles Police Department,
"Women in the LAPD," http://
www.lapdonline.org/history_of_
the_lapd/content_basic_view/833
(Accessed June 23, 2008).
3. Officer.com, "The Directory,"
http://www.officer.com/links/
Agency_Search (Accessed June 23,
2008).
4. *New York Magazine*, "9/11 by the
numbers," http://nymag.com/news/
articles/wtc/1year/numbers.htm
(Accessed June 23, 2008); National
Law Enforcement Officers Memorial Fund, http://www.nleomf.com/
TheMemorial/Facts/911deaths.htm.
5. Anthony DePalma, "Tracing Lung
Ailments that Rose with 9/11
Dust," *New York Times*, May 13,
2006.
6. Officer.com, "The Directory," http://
www.officer.com/links/Agency_
Search (Accessed June 23, 2008).
7. Seth Mydans, "The Police Verdict,"
New York Times, April 30, 1992.
8. National Geographic Channel,
"The Final Report: The L.A. Riots,"
Spike.com, http://www.spike.com/

tag/national-geographic-channel (Accessed June 23, 2008)

9. Curt Gentry, *J. Edgar Hoover: The Man and the Secrets* (New York: Plume, 1991), 415–17.

Chapter 4

1. Officer Down Memorial Page, "Honoring All Fallen Members of the New York State Police," http://www.odmp.org/agency/2768-new-york-state-police-new-york (Accessed October 16, 2009).

2. Texas Ranger Hall of Fame & Museum, http://www.texasranger.org/halloffame/Hamer_Frank.htm.

3. Officer.com, "The Directory," http://www.officer.com/links/Agency_Search (Accessed June 24, 2008).

4. Ibid.

5. Judith McDonough, "Worker Solidarity, Judicial Oppression, and Police Repression in the Westmoreland County, Pennsylvania Coal Miner's Strike, 1910-1911," *Pennsylvania History,* 64 (1997): 384–406.

6. Michael Newton, *The Ku Klux Klan* (Jefferson, N.C.: McFarland, 2007), 252–56, 322–23.

7. James Dickerson, *Dixie's Dirty Secret: The True Story of How the Government, the Media, and the Mob Conspired to Combat Integration and the Vietnam Antiwar Movement* (Armonk, N.Y.: M. E. Sharpe, 1998), 117; Jerry Mitchell, "Documents Show Klan Targeted Blacks, Whites," *Jackson* (Miss.) *Clarion Ledger,* November 25, 2008.

8. Fred Ferretti, "Autopsies Show Shots Killed 9 Attica Hostages, Not Knives; State Official Admits Mistake," *New York Times,* September 15, 1971; William Farrell, "Rockefeller Lays Hostages' Deaths to Troopers' Fire," *New York Times,* September 17, 1971; *New York Times,* "Use of Shotguns in Attica Revolt Deplored in House Unit's Report," June 27, 1973.

9. Jodi Wilgoren, "A Nation Challenged: The Detainees; Swept up in a Dragnet, Hundreds Sit in Custody and Ask, 'Why?'" *New York Times,* November 25, 2001.

10. Officer Down Memorial Page, "California Highway Patrol," http://www.odmp.org/agency/504-california-highway-patrol-california (Accessed October 16, 2009).

11. Lisa Rein, "Md. Police Put Activists' Names on Terror Lists," *Washington Post,* October 8, 2008; Tom Roberts, "'Terrorist' Nuns Spotlight Homeland Security," *National Catholic Reporter,* December 11, 2008; Robert Baer, "When the State Police Fingers Terrorists," *Time,* October 17, 2008, http://www.time.com/time/nation/article/0,8599,1850692,00.html (Accessed June 24, 2008); The Affirmative Action and Diversity Project "State Police Deny Labeling Michigan Groups as Terrorists," http://aad.english.ucsb.edu/docs/09-01-05AP.htm (Accessed June 24, 2008).

Chapter 5

1. U.S. Constitution, art. 6, cl. 2.

2. U.S. Marshals Service, "The First Generation of United States Marshals," http://www.usmarshals.gov/history/firstmarshals/marshals1.htm (Accessed June 24, 2008).

3. William Doyle, *An American Insurrection* (New York: Anchor, 2001), 280.

4. U.S. Marshals Service, "U.S. Marshals and the Pentagon Riot of October 21, 1967," http://www.usmarshals.gov/history/civilian/1967b.htm (Accessed June 24, 2008).

5. U.S. Marshals Service, "Witness Security Program," http://www.usmarshals.gov/witsec/index.html (Accessed June 24, 2008).

6. U.S. Marshals Service, "Operation FALCON: Federal and Local Cops Organized Nationally" http://www.usmarshals.gov/falcon/index.html (Accessed June 24, 2008).

7. U.S. Secret Service, "Secret Service History," http://www.secretservice.gov/history.shtml (Accessed June 24, 2008).

8. Michael Newton, *The FBI Encyclopedia* (Jefferson, N.C.: McFarland, 2003), 87.

9. Federal Bureau of Investigation, "History of the FBI—The New Deal: 1933-Late 1930's," http://www.fbi.gov/libref/historic/history/newdeal.htm (Accessed June 24, 2008).

10. Paul Shukovsky, Tracy Johnson, and Daniel Lathrop, "The FBI's Terrorism Trade-Off," *Seattle Post-Intelligencer,* April 11, 2007.

11. Ward Churchill and Jim Vander Wall, *The COINTELPRO Papers* (Boston: South End Press, 1990), 304.

12. Stephen Fox, *Blood and Power: Organized Crime in Twentieth-Century America* (New York: Penguin, 1989), 337.

13. Kathleen Downe, *Spirits of Defiance* (Columbus: University of Ohio Press, 2005), 35; Henry Lee, *How Dry We Were* (Englewood Cliffs, N.J.: Prentice-Hall, 1963), 6, 68, 162.

14. Mitchel Roth and James Olson, *Historical Dictionary of Law Enforcement* (Westport, Conn.: Greenwood, 2001), 170.

15. Drug Enforcement Administration, "DEA History," http://www.usdoj.gov/dea/history.htm (Accessed June 24, 2008).

16. Drug Enforcement Administration, "Stats & Facts," http://www.usdoj.gov/dea/statistics.html#seizures (Accessed June 24, 2008).

17. Officer.com, "The Directory," http://www.officer.com/links/Agency_Search (Accessed June 24, 2008).

18. Tennessee Valley Authority, "TVA Heritage." http://www.tva.gov/index.htm (Accessed June 24, 2008).

Chapter 6

1. Jens Gould, "Mexico Organized Crime Murder Toll for Year Passes 5,000 Mark," December 3, 2008, Blomberg.com, http://www.bloomberg.com/apps/news?pid=20601086&sid=aWaMjy7SQ2M4&refer=latin_america (Accessed June 24, 2008); Jerry Brewer, "Homicide Rate in Mexico is Appalling," Mexidata.info January 16, 2006, http://mexidata.info/id750.html (Accessed June 24, 2008).

2. Teresa Rodriguez and Diana Montané, *The Daughters of Juarez: A True Story of Serial Murder South of the Border* (New York: Atria, 2008), 148.

3. *International Herald Tribune,* "In Anti-Corruption Move, Mexico Forces Top Police to Prove

Trustworthiness or Lose Jobs," June 25, 2007.

4. Central Intelligence Agency, *The World Factbook,* https://www.cia.gov/library/publications/the-world-factbook/index.html (Accessed June 24, 2008).

5. Permanent Court of International Justice, "Publications of the Permanent Court of International Justice (1922-1946)," http://www.icj-cij.org/pcij/index.php?p1=9&PHPSESSID=1cc0ec4a64b5d24987e3c99d8f9f8cc2 (Accessed June 24, 2008).

6. Yale Law School, "The International Military Tribunal for Germany," http://avalon.law.yale.edu/subject_menus/imt.asp (Accessed June 24, 2008); Scrapbookpages.com, "American Military Tribunal at Dachau," http://www.scrapbook-pages.com/ DachauScrapbook/DachauTrials/Introduction.html (Accessed June 24, 2008); Memorial Hall of the Victims in the Nanjing Massacre, "The Tokyo War Crimes Trials," http://www.cnd.org/mirror/nanjing/NMTT.html (Accessed June 24, 2008); World War II Database, "The Tokyo Trial and Other Trials Against Japan," http://ww2db.com/battle_spec.php?battle_id=221 (Accessed June 24, 2008).

7. Interpol, "About Interpol," http://www.interpol.int/public/icpo/default.asp (Accessed June 24, 2008).

8. Jerry Garner, "Interpol Arrests Hundreds in Asian Sports Betting Sting," Associated Content, November 24, 2007, http://www.associatedcontent.com/article/457984/interpl_arrests_hundreds_in_asian.html (Accessed June 24, 2008).

9. Europol, "Europol at a Glance," http://www.europol.europa.eu/index.asp?page=ataglance&language= (Accessed June 24, 2008).

10. Europol, "Official Opening of Europol," http://www.europol.europa.eu/index.asp?page=news&news =pr991001.htm (Accessed June 24, 2008).

11. Europol, "Fact Sheet on Europol," http://www.europol.europa.eu/index.asp?page=facts (Accessed June 24, 2008).

12. Cornell University Law School Legal Information Institute, "U.S. Code Collection: TITLE 18 > PART II > CHAPTER 209 > §3181," http://www.law.cornell.edu/uscode/html/uscode18/usc_sec_18_00003181----000-notes.html (Accessed June 24, 2008).

13. "Israeli 'Hits' on Terrorists," Jewish Virtual Library, http://www.jewishvirtuallibrary.org/jsource/Terrorism/hits.html (Accessed June 24, 2008).

14. Richard Clarke, *Against All Enemies: America's War on Terror* (New York: Free Press, 2004), 143–4.

15. Jane Mayer, "Outsourcing Torture: The Secret History of America's 'Extraordinary Rendition' Program," *New Yorker,* http://www.newyorker.com/archive/2005/02/14/050214fa_fact6 (Accessed June 24, 2008).

16. Dana Priest, "Wrongful Imprisonment: Anatomy of a CIA Mistake," *Washington Post,* December 4, 2005.

17. Helen Thomas, "Bush Admits He Approved Torture," *Seattle Post-Intelligencer,* May 1, 2008.

18. Drug Enforcement Administration, "175 Alleged Gulf Cartel Members Arrested in Massive International Law Enforcement Operation," http://www.usdoj.gov/dea/pubs/pressrel/pr091708.html (Accessed June 24, 2008).

19. United Nations, "Rome Statute of the International Criminal Court," http://www.un.org/children/conflict/keydocuments/english/romestatuteofthe7.html (Accessed June 24, 2008).

20. International Criminal Court, "Situations and Cases," http://www.icc-cpi.int/Menus/ICC/Situations+and+Cases/ (Accessed October 16, 2009).

21. "Road Cleared for Start of ICC's Long-Delayed First Trial," Agence France-Presse, November 18, 2007, http://www.google.com/hostednews/afp/article/ALeqM5h9-G0ngqaMx513TRwakptt11ZrdCQ (Accessed June 24, 2008).

Chapter 7

1. Harry MacLean, *In Broad Daylight* (New York: Harper & Row, 1989)

2. Thomas Page, "The Real Judge Lynch," *Atlantic Monthly* (December 1901): 731–43.

3. Famous American Trials, "Lynchings: By Year and Race," http://www.law.umkc.edu/faculty/projects/ftrials/shipp/lynchingyear.html (Accessed June 26, 2008).

4. Richard Brown, "The American Vigilante Tradition," in *The History of Violence in America,* Hugh Graham and Ted Gurr, eds. (New York: Bantam, 1969), 154–226.

5. Allen Trelease, *White Terror* (New York: Harper & Row, 1971), 135.

6. Benjamin Stolberg, "Vigilantism, 1937," *The Nation* 145 (August 14, 1937): 166–8.

7. Richard Brown, 201–8.

8. National Crime Prevention Council, "Neighborhood Watch," http://www.ncpc.org/topics/neighborhood-watch (Accessed June 26, 2008).

9. Philip Ethington, "Vigilantes and the Police: The Creation of a Professional Police Bureaucracy in San Francisco, 1847–1900," *Journal of Social History* 21 (Winter 1987): 197–227.

10. William Sherman, *Memoirs of General William T. Sherman,* http://www.gutenberg.org/etext/4361 (Accessed June 26, 2008).

11. Richard Brown, 219.

12. Crime Stoppers International, "Our History," http://www.c-s-i.org/OurHistory.aspx (Accessed June 26, 2008).

13. Crime Stoppers International, http://www.c-s-i.org (Accessed June 26, 2008); Crime Stoppers USA, http://www.crimestopusa.com (Accessed June 26, 2008).

14. Crime Stoppers USA, "Scholastic Programs," http://www.crimestopusa.com/SchoolPrograms.asp (Accessed June 26, 2008).

15. National Association of Police Athletic/Activities Leagues, http://www.nationalpal.org (Accessed June 26, 2008).

16. National Association of Police Athletic/Activities Leagues, "About P.A.L.," http://www. nationalpal.org/index.php?option=com_frontpage&Itemid=1 (Accessed June 26, 2008).

17. Mothers Against Drunk Driving, "History," http://www.madd.org/About-us/About-us/History.aspx (Accessed June 26, 2008).

18. Guardian Angels, "Chapter List," http://www.guardianangels.org/safety_full.php (Accessed June 26, 2008).

19. International Alliance of Guardian Angels, *The Official Guardian Angels Training Book*, http://www.guardianangels.org/manual/pdf/2.pdf (Accessed October 16, 2009), 53.

20. CyberAngels, http://www.cyberangels.org/index.php (Accessed June 26, 2008).

21. National Highway Traffic Safety Administration, *Statistical Analysis of Alcohol-Related Driving Trends, 1982–2005* (Washington, D.C.: U.S. Department of Transportation, 2005), 2.

22. Tom Incantalupo, "'MADD: Device Key to Keep Drinkers Off Road," *Newsday*, November 21, 2006.

Chapter 8

1. Scott Ellsworth, *Death in a Promised Land* (Baton Rouge: Louisiana State University Press, 1982), 45–8.

2. Ellsworth, 51–3.

3. Ellsworth, 66–70.

4. A.D. Hopkins, "Man of the Years," *Las Vegas Review-Journal*, http://www.1st100.com/part2/webb.html (Accessed June 26, 2008).

5. Matthew Kerbel, *If It Bleeds, It Leads* (New York: Basic Books, 2000).

6. *New York Times*, "15 Were Injured by Bomb Blasts," January 23, 1957.

7. Ted Ottley, "Ted Kaczynski: The Unabomber," tru TV Crime Library http://www.trutv.com/library/crime/terrorists_spies/terrorists/kaczynski/1.html (Accessed October 16, 2009).

8. Ray Surette, "Self-Reported Copycat Crime among a Population of Serious and Violent Juvenile Offenders," *Crime & Delinquency* 48 (2002): 46–69.

9. Centre for Prevention of Suicide, *Music and Suicide* (Alberta: Canadian Mental Health Association, 1989), 1.

10. Federal Bureau of Investigation, "New Top Ten Fugitive," http://www.fbi.gov/page2/nov08/topten_112908.html (Accessed June 26, 2008).

11. Marilyn Bardsley, "Son of Sam," tru TV Crime Library, http://www.trutv.com/library/crime/serial_killers/notorious/berkowitz/letter_1.html (Accessed June 26, 2008).

12. *America's Most Wanted*, "Notorious AMW Fugitive John List Dead at 82," http://www.amw.com/features/feature_story_detail.cfm?id=2613 (Accessed October 6, 2009).

13. U.S. Marshals Service, "Fugitive Investigations," http://www.usmarshals.gov/investigations/index.html (Accessed June 26, 2008).

14. Free Public Records Finder, "Most Wanted Persons/Fugitives," http://www.freeprf.com/wanted.html (Accessed June 26, 2008).

15. America's Most Wanted, "End of the Line for Mark Everett," http://www.amw.com/fugitives/brief.cfm?id=28521 (Accessed June 26, 2008).

16. *Larry King Live*, "Interview with John Walsh," CNN, December 27, 2001, http://transcripts.cnn.com/TRANSCRIPTS/0112/27/lkl.00.html (Accessed June 26, 2008).

Bibliography

Chaliand, Gérard, and Arnaud Blin. *The History of Terrorism: From Antiquity to al Qaeda*. Berkeley: University of California Press, 2007.

Fooner, Michael. *Interpol: The Inside Story of the International Crime-Fighting Organization*. Washington, D.C.: Henry Regnery, 1973.

———. *Women in Policing: Fighting Crime around the World*. New York: Putnam, 1976.

Fox, Stephen. *Blood and Power: Organized Crime in 20th-Century America*. New York: Penguin, 1990.

Lauder, Ronald. *Fighting Violent Crime in America*. New York: Dodd Mead, 1985.

Newton, Michael. *The Encyclopedia of High-Tech Crime and Crime-Fighting*. New York: Facts on File, 2004.

———. *The FBI Encyclopedia*. Jefferson, N.C.: McFarland, 2004.

Sterling, Claire. *Thieves' World: The Threat of the New Global Network of Organized Crime*. New York: Simon & Schuster, 1994.

Further Resources

Print

Flint, Scott, Grant Flint, and Chris Thompson. *Waking the Tiger Within: How to Be Safe from Crime on the Street, at Home, on Trips, at Work, and at School.* Philadelphia: Parthenon Press, 2007.

Parker, Donna. *Fighting Computer Crime: A New Framework for Protecting Information.* Hoboken, N.J.: Wiley, 1998.

Schwabe, William. *Challenges and Choices for Crime-Fighting Technology: Federal Support of State and Local Law Enforcement.* Santa Monica, Calif.: RAND Corporation, 2001.

Internet

Europol
http://www.europol.europa.eu

Federal Bureau of Investigation
http://www.fbi.gov

International Association of Chiefs of Police
http://www.theiacp.org

Interpol
http://www.interpol.int

Index

About the Author

Michael Newton has published 215 books since 1977, with 21 forthcoming from various houses through 2011. His history of the Florida Ku Klux Klan (*The Invisible Empire,* 2001) won the Florida Historical Society's 2002 Rembert Patrick Award for "Best Book in Florida History," and his *Encyclopedia of Cryptozoology* was one of the American Library Association's Outstanding Reference Works in 2006. His nonfiction work includes 13 previous volumes for Facts on File and Checkmark.